THE HEART OF RAHNER

THE HEART OF
RAHNER

LONDON
BURNS & OATES

First published by Burns & Oates 1980. Chosen and arranged by John Griffiths. Translations by divers hands. Arrangement of text and translations copyright© Search Press Limited 1980. All rights reserved. No part of this book may be reproduced, stored in a retrieval system, transmitted or recorded in any form or by any means known or yet to be invented for any purpose whatsoever without the written permission of the publishers, Burns & Oates, 2-10 Jerdan Place, London SW6 5PT.

ISBN 0-86012-099-6 (UK)

Set in IBM 11/12 pt. Baskerville by 𝔽 Tek-Art, Croydon, Surrey
Printed and bound in Great Britain by
Camelot Press, Southampton

CONTENTS

HOLY SPIRIT

Everything that we are prays in us for the Holy Spirit of the Father and of the Son. The recognition that we are outcasts before God, our weakness—even our sinfulness, which causes us to lose God's word through carelessness, our poverty, weakness and darkness, even our coldness towards God and his holy love—everything that is in us prays in mute expectancy for the Holy Spirit of the Father and of the Son.

Come, Spirit, Spirit of the Father and of the Son. Come, Spirit of love, Spirit of sonship, Spirit of peace, of faith, of strength, of holy joy. Come, secret joy, into the tears of the world. Come, victory-rich life, into the death of the earth. Come, Father of the poor, support of the oppressed. Come, Love, who is poured out into our hearts. We have nothing that can force you; yet on that very account we are confident. Our hearts stand in mysterious awe at your coming, because you are selfless and gentle, because you are something else than our heart. Yet this is for us the firmest promise that you are nevertheless coming. Come, therefore, come to us every day, again and again. We put our trust in you. Where else could we trust? We love you because you are love itself. In you we have God for our Father, because you cry out in us, 'Abba, Father'. We thank you, quickening Spirit, Holy Spirit, we thank you for dwelling in us, for having willed to be in us the seal of the living God, the seal that stamps us as his property. Do not forsake us in the bitter struggle that is life; do not forsake us at the end when everything else will abandon us.

1

HOPE OF ETERNITY

We ask you, God of grace and eternal life, to increase and strengthen hope in us. Give us this virtue of the strong, this power of the confident, this courage of the unshakable. Make us always have a longing for you, the infinite plenitude of being. Make us always build on you and your fidelity, always hold fast without despondency to your might. Make us to be of this mind and produce this attitude in us by your Holy Spirit. Then, our Lord and God, we shall have the virtue of hope. Then we can courageously set about the task of our life again and again. Then we shall be animated by the joyful confidence that we are not working in vain. Then we shall do our work in the knowledge that in us and through us and, where our powers fail, without us, you the almighty according to your good pleasure are working to your honour and our salvation. Strengthen your hope in us.

The hope of eternity, however, eternal God, is your only begotten Son. He possesses your infinite nature from eternity to eternity, because you have communicated it to him and ever communicate it, in eternal generation. He therefore possesses all that we hope and desire. He is wisdom and power, beauty and goodness, life and glory, he is all in all. And he, this Son to whom you have given all, has become ours. He became man. Your eternal Word, God of glory, became man, became like one of us, humbled himself and took human form, a human body, a human soul, a human life, a human lot even in its most terrible possibilities. Your Son, heavenly Father, truly became man. We kneel in adoration. For who can measure this incomprehensible love of yours? You have loved the world so much that men take offence at your love and call the affirmation of the incarnation of your Son folly and madness. But we believe in the incomprehensibility, the overwhelming audacity of your love. And because we believe, we can exult in blessed hope: Christ in us is the hope of glory. For if you give us your Son, what can there be you have held back, what can there be which you have refused us? If we possess your Son to whom you have given everything, your own substance, what could still be lacking to us? And he is truly ours. For he is the Son of Mary, who is our sister in Adam, he is a child of Adam's family, of the same race as we are, one in substance and origin with man. And if we human beings in your plans and according to your will as creator are all to form a great community of descent and destiny, and if your Son is to belong to this one great community, then we, precisely we poor children of Eve, share the race and lot of your own Son. We are brothers of the only-begotten, the brethren of your Son, co-heirs of his glory. We share in his grace, in his Spirit, in his life, in his destiny through cross and glorification, in his eternal glory. It is no longer *we* who live our life but Christ our brother lives his life in us and through us. We are ready, Father of Jesus Christ and our Father, to share in the life of your Son. Dispose of our life, make it confortable to the life of your Son. He wills to continue his own life in us until the end of time, he wills to reveal in us and in our life the glory, the greatness, beauty and the blessed power of his life. What meets us in life is not chance, is not blind fate but is a part of the life of your Son. The joy we shall receive as Christ's joy, success as his success, pain as his pain, sorrow as his sorrow, work as his work, death as a sharing in his death.

In one respect we ask especially for your grace. Make us share in Jesus' prayer. He is the great worshipper of God in spirit and in truth, he is the mediator through whom alone our prayer can reach to the throne of grace. We wish to pray in him, united with his prayer. May he, with whom we are united in his Spirit, teach us to pray. May he teach us to pray as he himself prayed, to pray at all times and not to slacken, to pray perseveringly, confidently, humbly, in spirit and in truth, with true love of our neighbour without which no prayer is pleasing to you. May he teach us to pray for what he prayed: that your name may be hallowed, your will be done, your Kingdom come to us, for only if we first pray in that way for your honour will you also hear us if we pray for ourselves, our earthly well-being and earthly cares. Give us the spirit of prayer, of recollection, of union with God. Lord accept my poor heart. It is often so far from you. It is like a waste land without water, lost in the innumerable things and trifles that fill my everyday life. Only you, Lord, can focus my heart on you, who are the centre of all hearts and the Lord of every soul. Only you can give the spirit of prayer, only your grace is capable of granting me to find you through the multiplicity of things and the distraction of mind of everyday routine, you the one thing necessary, the one thing in which my heart can rest. May your Spirit come to the help of my weakness, and when we do not know what we should ask, may he intercede for us with inexpressible sighs, and you who know men's hearts will hear what your Spirit interceding for us desires in us.

Finally, however, I ask you for the hardest and most difficult, for the grace to recognize the cross of your Son in all the suffering of my life, to adore your holy and inscrutable will in it, to follow your Son on his way to the cross as long as it may please you. Make me sensitive in what concerns your honour and not merely for my own well-being, and then I also will be able to carry many a cross as atonement for my sins. Do not let me be embittered by suffering but mature, patient, selfless, gentle and filled

4

with longing for that land where there is no pain and for that day when you will wipe all tears from the eyes of those who have loved you and in sorrow have believed in your love and in darkness have believed in your light. Let my pain be a profession of my faith in your promises, a profession of my hope in your goodness and fidelity, a profession of my love, that I love you more than myself, that I love you for your own sake even without reward. May the cross of my Lord be my model, my power, my consolation, the solution of all obscure questions, the light of every darkness. Grant that we may glory in the cross of our Lord Jesus Christ, grant us to become so mature in true Christian being and life that we no longer regard the cross as a misfortune and incomprehensible meaninglessness but as a sign of your election, as the secret, sure sign that we are yours for ever. For it is a faithful saying that if we die with him we shall also live with him and if we endure with him, we shall also reign with him. Father, we will to share everything with your Son, his life, his divine glory and therefore his suffering and his death. Only with the cross, give the strength to bear it. Cause us to experience in the cross its blessing also. Give us the cross which your wisdom knows is for our salvation and not our ruin.

Son of the Father, Christ who lives in us, you are our hope of glory. Live in us, bring our life under the laws of your life, make our life like to yours. Live in me, pray in me, suffer in me, more I do not ask. For if I have you I am rich; those who find you have found the power and the victory of their life. Amen.

PRAYER

Prayer is *the* great religious act. What man really is in the depths of his being, something that cannot be static but must be realized in a fundamental activity in time yet transcending time, that is prayer. It is the acceptance of the prime fact of being created, not in stupor of resignation, but alert to his coming from the Father's hands. It is committing oneself to the basic dynamism of the kernel of the person, wishing in a way to break through all limits of time and space, but still seeing its fulfilment not in infinite being, but in the Thou who speaks and answers and first calls. It is the all-pervasive longing for happiness, not seeking emotional satisfaction but personal fulfilment. It is the will to free action, which ultimately can only be realized in face of a person who is immanent to all possibilities of freedom and summons man to freedom. In a word, it is unconditional and therefore sensitive openness to the God who transcends all the encounters of everyday life but who uses them and goes beyond them to demand an answer to the basic question of our existence, the meaning of life. Hence tradition tries to define prayer as the 'ascent to God' and Scripture speaks of 'pouring out the soul before God' (1 Sam 1.15), of longing for God 'as the hart longs for flowing streams' (Ps 42.1), of lifting up the heart (Ps 25.1), of taking refuge in the Lord (Ps 31.1f.). In modern terminology it can become man's self-commitment to the transcendence of his own being, hence the humble, receptive and reverent admission of, and the reactive, responsive affirmative dedication to his call and destiny, the impact of the mystery of God as person on human existence, to which man cannot but be somehow sensible.

But it is equally important to recall the simple description of prayer as the great art of conversing with Jesus (*Imitation of Christ*, II, 8). It is like Abraham's negotiations with Yahweh (Gen 18.23-33) which strike us as very anthropomorphic, or the dialogue of our Lord in Gethsemane as he wrestles with the will of his Father, or the encounters with

God of which we read in the lives or legends of the saints, and which we find so overfamiliar as almost to seem blasphemous. While the first definition strives to convey the majesty and universal omnipotence of God, the definition of prayer as 'speaking to God' bears on the truth that God hears 'me', that he has chosen 'me' very personally, and that 'my' casual steps are guided by his infinite wisdom. This truth is operative above all in the prayer of petition. The attempt to make abandonment to God's providence the quintessence of prayer ignores its character of dialogue. It stresses one truth, the immutability of God (which taken in isolation would mean that real prayer is impossible) and forgets the other, that God is 'personally' concerned with our affairs. The immutability of God must not be reduced to a proposition which can be manipulated in the usual categories of human thought. It must be kept open for the truth of the incarnation and crucifixion, for the truth that God 'changes' for the sake of man. This is the only possible source of a dialogal character of prayer.

In true Christian prayer, the granting or refusal of requests is not a problem. One need only think of the typical pilgrimage where the believer whose request has not been granted in spite of or because of his ardent prayer still gains the profound peace of answered prayer. This may be illustrated by an analogy from personal relationships. Any genuine request is always put forward as the minor wish in which the general plea for the other's favour is crystallized. But the Christain prayer of petition takes its impetus (i.e., has its certainty of being heard) from the saving gift of God to men, which is Jesus Christ.

If prayer then spans the whole distance between ascent to God and dialogue with God, its basic forms—adoration, praise, thanksgiving, petition, repentance, sacrifice, and so on—are seen to be its natural connotations. Adoration is undoubtedly closer to the 'ascent', but without dialogal encounter there can be no adoration, just as there can be no genuine petition without the inward impulse of the Spirit of God, such as is expressed in the *sursumactio*.

This span is wide enough to take in much that is often too quickly rejected in the phenomenology of religion as un-Christian. Christian prayer, is which the intrinsic tension is again surpassed in the person of the Lord, who is God, filling all things while remaining the same, the man, limited and changing historically, appears even phenomenologically as the climax and fulfilment of the prayer of the nations. And this does not mean that non-Christian prayer must be at once branded as un-Christian non-prayer.

The first essential component follows at once from what has been said. Prayer is a grace, a gift of God, a response to something which was previously put on man's lips and in his heart. But prayer is also man's own free act. To have some idea of this mystery, we must first distinguish the aspect of what is given by God from the aspect of what is accomplished by man's own force.

All prayer is wholly the gift of God. There is nothing in it that we can keep for ourselves. There is no previous foothold that we can provide for God's action, and no later response that we can give of ourselves. But prayer is likewise human action. Man is not a machine kept in motion by God. He is free, and there can be no question of prayer unless it is rooted in man's freedom, an action for which he is personally responsible. These two aspects, which both take in the total act of human prayer, must be clearly distinguished. Only then can we truly admire the new mystery, that prayer is after all a response to the call of God, that, cutting across the different levels, divine grace and human freedom still meet. This has been the bliss of great saints, often experienced in fear and trembling. But this

8

interplay of call and response is at the heart of all prayer, even the prayer of petition, whose structure only seems to be different when it is considered superficially.

Prayer is also a unity of the inward and outer man. Man prays when he is inwardly and outwardly recollected, when he is himself. 'Interior prayer' always seeks to express itself in word and gesture, while 'external' or vocal prayer can influence the inner attitude when one is tired and distracted. The traditional distinction between 'attention' and 'intention' is irrelevant here, and this is one way to understand the rosary (though there are also other approaches). But the practical consequences are more important. Prayer must of course aim at being 'interior' but since man lives in the external world it must also be guided by external rules, postures and formulas and follow the cycle of feast-days and times for prayer.

The importance of the link between the inner and the outer appears plainly in the third essential factor: prayer is always both individual and social. The theological reason for this is the unity of the Spirit, who is the Spirit of the Church and also animates each of the faithful. The Christian has both to praise God in a fellowship of prayer and formulate his own prayer for himself. But he must not forget that the prayer of the individual relies on the community which it serves, and that the only ultimate meaning of community prayer is to lead the individual to God. There can be no problems of precedence here, since each man is, irreducibly, at the same time both an individual called personally by God and part of the chain of mankind whose link with God is Jesus Christ. The closer it is to the Eucharist, the centre of prayer in common, the higher the degree of unity in prayer. The breviary is prayer in common in its own way, as are also congregational devotions. The same principle of social prayer also explains, for instance, the precept of going to Mass on Sundays, and the duty of praying for parents and relations. The notion of proclaiming fellowship before God can throw new light on a feature of the early Church, prayer as a confession of faith, which in turn may throw new light on pilgrimages and so on.

A further basic structure of prayer follows from the link between prayer and words, which in its highest form is identity. Language is the real personal bond of fellowship. It is the most perfect expression of the inward man. Language here means simply that the Word became flesh and encounters us in the word of Scripture and the articulate action of the sacraments. It is only today that this dominant role of language is coming into view. If prayer is really the basic religious act and the verbalization (its personal outcome) is not merely a vehicle of prayer but its essence—prayer is speaking to God—we can measure the responsibility of those who have to deal with the words. The verbal character also throws light on prayer as a confession of faith, since all honest language is at once the giving of testimony.

The demands bring out one further quality, that prayer falls short of what it should really do. This is not a matter of sin, though closely connected with it, nor of incidentals which might be avoided, say, by greater recollection. Man, as he encounters God, is at once conscious of his darkness before the radiant light. Man essentially receives at prayer, and prayer with all the due reserves made above, is essentially a process of receiving. It has often been experienced as such by great men of prayer, who saw their own poverty better the more gifts they received. The prayer, 'Lord I am not worthy' is not just for beginners but also—to keep to the terminology— for the perfect. Penitential prayer, adoration and many other forms must be interpreted in the light of this principle.

Essentially, prayer is the explicit and positive realization of our natural and supernatural relationship with the personal God of salvation. It realizes the essence of the religious act. It is man's entry into the transcendence of his own being, in which he allows himself to become receptive, humble and reverent, gives himself in a positive response, and is totally available and subjectively concerned in his whole existence with the mystery of God as a person. All positive religious acts which are directly and explicitly related, both knowingly and willingly, to God may be called prayer. Even sacrifice is essentially no more than prayer made objective by external presentation. The *a priori,* integral, rational, personal, categorical and incarnate structures of the religious act are therefore structures of prayer. As a response, Christian prayer is an acceptance of the transcendence directed towards the God of eternal life which is made known in grace by God's revelation of himself. It is therefore essentially an act of faith and hope which is fulfilled (when it is fully expressed) in total surrender to the love of God. It is therefore an act of salvation, borne by the grace of the Spirit, having God 'in' Christ in view. Whether prayer is always an act of virtue of religion depends on our definition of the concept of religion. In other words, it depends on whether this is simply concerned with external acts of worship as such or whether it is concerned with full, inner worship of God. Insofar as prayer is an act of grace and is therefore 'in Christ', it is also prayer 'in Christ and in the Church' (see Eph. 3.21) and therefore it has an ecclesiological character. This character is of course much more explicit in the official liturgy of the Church and as such liturgical prayer, at least under similar circumstances, is more valuable and more effective. The commandment to love one's neighbour implies a duty to pray, at least in general, for one's fellow men.

11

Apart from the fact that we may and indeed must, as created beings with a need to care for ourselves that is recognized and wanted by God, pray for ourselves and for our own salvation, prayer also has, as an act of divine virtue, its own intentionality which in itself and for its own sake tends towards God. Because the man who prays forgets himself in this way and does not wish to assert himself, his prayer will inevitably be anthropocentric in the right sense. It will also have the objective merit, which is not sought as the first and the most all-embracing motive for prayer, of being a good work and an act of salvation. It will also lead to an increase of grace. It will similarly have the effect of satisfaction. A theological distinction is made between this and the 'impenetrative' effect of the prayer of petition as a request for God's mercy. Prayer must have all the qualities possessed by the virtues of faith, hope and love—certainty, firmness and radical self-surrender. Just as there are saving acts which prepare for justification by preventive grace, so too is there the prayer of the penitent sinner and this is also a necessary disposition for justification. As a realization of man's being which is orientated towards God in dialogue and which God wished to create and to perfect by grace, true prayer is pleasing to God and acceptable to him; it is not merely anthropomorphic. As man's asking for God (a petition that is borne up by God's act itself) and for everything else only insofar as it forms part of this aspiring for God in accordance with God's unconditionally accepted plan, prayer is certainly heard by God. It is, moreover, heard whether we pray for ourselves or for others although, even in prayer of the right kind, the way in which it is heard is left to God. Insofar as it is the prayer of faith in the grace of Christ (whether this is consciously and reflectively known or not) for salvation in Christ, all authentic prayer is made 'in the name of Christ'. Since prayer is fundamentally no more than the concrete realization of the religious act, it hardly needs to be said not only that it is a necessary means of salvation (at least for the mature believer), but also that its content as a necessary religious act can also be as clear or as indistinct as faith itself as a necessary means of salvation may also possibly be under certain circumstances. The necessity of prayer gives a concrete form to the need for an explicit and positive orientation of man's whole life towards God. This also determines its extent and presence—it is always practised wherever the explicit orientation towards God is threatened or suppressed. Because of the integral structure of every religious act, oral prayer (including the use of fixed formulae of prayer) has a positive meaning, so long as we are totally orientated towards God in every aspect of our being when praying in this way. It is possible to make a distinction between the individual types of prayer only in their various ways of making the realization (which is implicit in every saving act) of man's raising of himself in supernatural transcendence towards God concrete in different explicit categories. These different kinds of prayer are, however, essentially the same. (This is also true of the prayer of petition, whenever it is an authentic and absolute surrender to God's will; similarly, every prayer of man in his need is always a prayer of petition, even when that man is praising and giving thanks to God, since God is always asked, in prayer, for God.) Prayer to the saints is, correctly understood, a very complex reality. It is a legitimate 'veneration' of the saints, a legitimate petition for their intercession and a realization in this form of prayer of a fundamental intention directed towards God. It is therefore a realization of the being of God, since it is always God who really hears this prayer to the saints. Insofar as it is implicitly an orientation towards God, every saving act is really also prayer, although this does not mean that formal prayer, as an explicit raising of the heart to God, is superfluous.

ADVENT

God has already begun to celebrate his advent in the world and in me. Softly and gently, so softly that it is possible to miss him, he has already taken the world and its world-time to his heart. He has put his own inconceivable life into this time of ours. We call that victory over fear of fleeting time, the grace of faith. And faith recognizes that God made this dying time in order to redeem it by taking it into his own eternity. There is an eternal now in us that has no nothingness any more: neither a nothingness past nor a nothingness to come. That *now* has already begun to collect our earthly moments and to take them into itself.

We do not rejoice with loud rejoicing in this Advent season. It lasts a lifetime, after all, and it makes such insistent demands on our poor hearts. There is no great rejoicing for we still feel, all too surely, the burdensome chains of time upon us. But within ourselves we ought to feel something living: the calm and modest joy of faithful hope which does not think that the graspable visible present is all that there is. That quiet joy is what a prisoner feels when he is still in his cell but is about to stand up, for he knows that the lock hangs loose at his cell door and that his freedom is certain. Is this joy, our Advent joy, so very hard to bear?

I AM YOUR LIFE

The feast of Christmas is not poetry and childish romanticism, but the avowal and the faith, which alone justifies man, that God has risen up and has already spoken his final word in the drama of history, no matter how much clamor the world keeps up. The celebration of Christmas can only be the echo of that word in the depth of our being by which we speak a believing Amen to God's word that has come from his vast eternity into the narrowness of this world, and yet has not ceased to be the word of God's truth and the word of his own blissful love. When not only the glimmer of candles, the joy of children and the fragrance of the Christmas tree but the heart itself answers God's childlike word of love with a gracious Yes, then Christmas really takes place, not only in mood, but in the most un-alloyed reality. For this word of the heart is then truly produced by God's holy grace; God's word is then born in our heart, too. God himself then moves into our heart, just as he moved into the world in Bethlehem, just as truly and really, and yet even more intimately. When the heart itself answers, we really open its gates high and wide, and God comes and takes possession of our hearts, just as in the first Christmas he came and took possession of the world.

And now he says to us what he has already said to the world as a whole through his grace-filled birth: 'I am there. I am with you. I am your life. I am your time. I am the gloom of your daily routine. Why will you not bear it? I weep your tears—pour yours out to me, my child. I am your joy. Do not be afraid to be happy, for ever since I wept, joy is the standard of living that is really more suitable than the anxiety and grief of those who think they have no hope. I am the blind alleys of all your paths, for when you no longer know how to go any further, then you have reached me, foolish child, though you are not aware of it. I am in your anxiety, for I have shared it by suffering it. And in doing so, I wasn't even heroic according to the wisdom of the world. I am in the prison of your finiteness, for my love has made me your prisoner. When the sums of

15

your plans and of your life's experiences do not balance out evenly, I am the unsolved remainder. And I know that this remainder, which makes you so frantic, is in reality my love, that you do not yet understand. I am present in your needs. I have suffered them and they are now transformed, but not obliterated from my heart. I am in your lowest fall, for today I began to descend into hell. I am in your death, for today I began to die with you, because I was born, and I have not let myself be spared any real part of this death.

'Do not be sorry, as Job was, for those who are born; for all who accept my salvation are born in this holy night because my Christmas embraces all your days and all your nights. I myself—my whole being and my whole personality —are truly engaged in the terrifying adventure that begins with your birth. I tell you, mine was no easier and no less dangerous than yours. I assure you, though, it had a happy ending. Ever since I became your brother, you are as near to me as I am to myself. If, therefore, I, as a creature, want to prove in me and in you, my brothers and sisters, that I, as Creator, have not made a hopeless experiment with the human race, who then shall tear my hand away from you? I accepted you when I took my human life to myself. As one of your kind, as a fresh start, I conquered in my failure.'

SAVING DESCENT

When we stand in faith before the Child's crib, we have to see that it is here that the decline called death begins, that descent which alone saves because its emptiness is filled with the unutterable inconceivability of God, which alone answers all the questions posed by our life in a thousand little ways. It answers them by surpassing them. Of course the death referred to here is always death redeemed by God, death fulfilled by God, which in our perspective is the descent of our existence and in God's perspective the ascent of God in what we call the Resurrection. Christmas is the beginning of that redeemed death and in any real sense can be understood only in that light.

The light of Christmas and the angels' carolling in praise of God, and their proclamation to men of an ultimate reconciliation through the grace of God must shine and resound in the depth of our death, or they will not be seen or heard. Christmas is not a feast of consolation that rescues us for a few uplifting moments from an incomprehensible fate. We celebrate Christmas where we are alive, in our movement towards death, and we do that because Jesus' birth was the beginning of his death.

WHAT IS MAN?

What do we mean by man? My reply, stripped to its essentials, is simple: Man is the question to which there is no answer.

THE STAR IS SHINING

Let us step forth on the adventurous journey of the heart to God! Let us run! Let us forget what lies behind us. The whole future lies open to us. Every possibility of life is still open, because we can still find God, still find more. Nothingness is over and done with for him who runs to meet God, the God whose smallest reality is greater than our boldest illusion, the God who is eternal youth and in whose country there dwells no resignation. We roam through the wilderness. Heart, do not despair over the sight of the

17

pilgrimage of men who, stooped over with the burden of their suppressed terror, march on and on, everyone, so it seems, with the same aimlessness. Do not despair. The star is there and it shines. The holy books tell where the Redeemer is to be found. Ardent restlessness urges us on. Speak to yourself! Doesn't the star stand still in the firmament of your heart? It is small? It is far away? But it is there! It is small only because you still have so far to go! It is far away only because your generosity is thought capable of an infinite journey. But the star is there! Even the *yearning* of the inner man for freedom, for goodness, for bliss, even the *regret* that we are weak, sinful men—these, too, are stars. Why do you yourself push clouds in front of the star—the clouds of bad temper, of disappointment, of bitterness, of refusal, clouds of sneering or of giving up— because your dreams and expectations have not been realized?

ONLY IN LOVE

What a poor creature you have made me, O God! All I know about you and about myself is that you are the eternal mystery of my life. Lord, what a frightful puzzle man is! He belongs to you, and you are the Incomprehensible—Incomprehensible in your being, and even more-so in your ways and judgments. For if all your dealings with me are acts of your freedom, quite unmerited gifts of your grace which knows no 'why,' if my creation and my whole life hang absolutely on your free decision, if all my paths are, after all, your paths and, therefore, unsearchable, then, Lord, no amount of questioning will ever fathom your depths—you will still be the Incomprehensible, even when I see you face to face.

18

But if you were not incomprehensible, you would be inferior to me, for my mind could grasp and assimilate you. You would belong to me, instead of I to you. And that would truly be hell, if I should belong only to myself! It would be the fate of the damned, to be doomed to pace up and down for all eternity in the cramped and confining prison of my own finiteness.

But can it be that you are my true home? Are you the one who will release me from my narrow little dungeon? Or are you merely adding another torment to my life, when you throw open the gates leading out upon your broad and endless plain? Are you anything more than my own great insufficiency, if all my knowledge leads only to your Incomprehensibility? Are you merely eternal unrest for the restless soul? Must every question fall dumb before you, unanswered? Is your only response the mute 'I will have it so', that so coldly smothers my burning desire to understand?

But I am rambling on like a fool—excuse me, God. You have told me through your Son that you are the God of my love, and you have commanded me to love you. Your commands are often hard because then enjoin the opposite of what my own inclinations would lead me to do, but when you bid me love you, you are ordering something that my own inclinations would never even dare to suggest: to love *you*, to come intimately close to you, to love your very life. You ask me to lose myself in you, knowing that you will take me to your heart, where I may speak on loving, familiar terms with you, the incomprehensible mystery of my life. And all this because you are love itself.

Only in love can I find you, my God. In love the gates of my soul spring open, allowing me to breathe a new air of freedom and forget my own petty self. In love my whole being streams forth out of the rigid confines of narrowness

19

and my own poverty and emptiness. In love all the powers of my soul flow out toward you, wanting never more to return, but to lose themselves completely in you, since by your love you are the inmost centre of my heart, closer to me than I am myself.

But when I love you, when I manage to break out of the narrow circle of self and leave behind the restless agony of unanswered questions, when my blinded eyes no longer look merely from afar and from the outside upon your unapproachable brightness, and much more when you yourself, incomprehensible one, have become through love the inmost centre of my life, then I can bury myself entirely in you, mysterious God, and with myself all my questions.

Love such as this wills to possess you as you are—how could it desire otherwise? It wants you yourself, not your reflection in the mirror of its own spirit. It wants to be united with you alone, so that in the very instant in which it gives up possession of itself, it will have not just your image, but your very self.

Love wants you as you are, and just as love knows that it itself is right and good and needs no further justification, so you are right and good for it, and it embraces you without asking for any explanation of why you are as you are. Your 'I will have it so' is love's greatest bliss. In this state of joy my mind no longer tries to bring you forcibly down to its level, in order to wrest from you your eternal secret, but rather love seizes me and carries me up to your level, into you.

LOVE, THE WORLD, AND THE CHURCH

How do we Christians picture the world—what we are and experience, with all that thus belongs to us? As one, vast, all-embracing, all-distinguishing event: the self-communication of God. God whom none can call by name, none comprehend, so that all we say of him must fall short of that incomprehensibility, that unspeakable abyss which sweeps everything away into its blinding darkness. But this God is our concern. It is he who penetrates the labyrinth of our minds, encompasses the realm of our experience with his mystery of morning and evening, is already existent before our own beginnings and yet remains eternally remote even when we have reached the end of all our ways in pursuit of him, and sink exhausted to the earth. We must always reckon with him, we must call on him though we can give him no name, and when we present our final reckoning, he must be there to ensure that there is a remainder, that we do not end in nothing.

We say of this God that the world is the event of his self-communication, the ecstasy of his love that would lavish itself outwardly on that which he is not. The tremendous outburst of his love, already sufficient to itself, creates from nothingness a world on which it can freely lavish itself. God's love, which in its eternal glory needs nothing, creates not so as to guide the world as an external force by remote control in the elliptical orbits of finitude, but in order to entrust himself to *his* world, thus letting it become the fate of divine love.

This love beggars comprehension. Judging by the forms in which it manifests itself, one might think it a monstrous blind force. It calls forth aeons and worlds apparently only to let them subside again into the void; it allows the absurdity of culpable denial of itself to enter its creation;

it quickens and kills, seems indifferent to individual beings, acts often as naked force, is deaf to the despairing cry of the oppressed and the ghastly rattle of the dying, is blind to the innocent helplessness of children that moves even our hardened hearts. But this love, that like the tidal wave of an infinite ocean roars through all space and time, uprooting everything, sweeping everything away, creates the material world and its tremendous evolution so as to make spirit, and the history of spirit, in it and of it. For after all, because of its essential orientation to spirit the material world is sustained from the outset by the creative dynamism which has as its goal the history of personal freedom, of which the material world is one element, intrinsic or extrinsic.

If this spirit is created and thrust into an immeasurable, free, open history, it is so that God can communicate his very self, so that in contact with the world he who always is may become what he always is: the ecstasy of love, which though it overburdens us, has made us such that only under this burden, which *is* love, can we be happy, though we can also forfeit this love by renouncing it in deadly sin. This totally incomprehensible God is the future, literally open to infinity itself, in the form of unfettered and immeasurable love, that knows no other law but itself. It does all things, suffers all things, permits all things, so that it may embrace all things in itself, descend into every abyss, break above every mountain-top, and triumph in all things and over all things, by lavishing itself on men and causing them to accept it as God's one mystery.

This love has a temporal history and is the driving force behind the history of this world; but it is not merely the hidden spring in the world's remotest depths, it also wishes to be manifested in the world's events and in people, in human love, in free acts, in sacrifice unto death, in faith,

22

hope, charity, whatever forms these may assume in the space and time that is our history. And the nearer this one history, sustained by God's self-communicating love, draws to the ultimate goal where this love will be 'all in all', victoriously consuming all things—provided a man has not rejected it outright—the more unmistakable its manifestation in history will be. Love has already found the predestined shape of its victory; even now the world's history unfolds not only by virtue of self-communicating love but also within the time of victory made manifest, the time of Jesus Christ, who unites within himself the radical, historical manifestation of God's definitive gift of himself to the world, and the world's acceptance of that gift.

The history of man flows on in the time of Christ that will never pass; but even in its historical manifestation it is encompassed by God's victorious self-gift. Indeed this manifestation has become history even more radically, history even within the world of steadily widening prospects; it is the history of man active in a hominization of the world and a self-manipulation of man on a scale yet undreamed of. And it is still a history that seems to man a growing chaos—an impenetrable maze of sin and holiness, light and darkness; a history of simultaneous ascents and downfalls, of blood and tears, of noble achievements and rash presumption; a history that is appalling and magnificent, an ooze of endless trivia and yet a high drama; a history in which the individual is freed from the degradation of self-alienation and is reduced to the status of total insignificance among the billions of his fellow men; a history of arrogant might and the inexorable demands of 'planning', yet increasingly unpredictable, with a glowing pluralism of cultures, economic systems, political systems; an ever more variegated human consciousness, and trends towards a society of the masses; so that this pluralism,

23

with all the schizophrenia it begets in the consciousness of the individual, is compressed into a highly inflammable density by a human history ever more closely-knit, ever more one.

In the midst of all this history, at a thousand different times and places, in a thousand forms, the one thing occurs which produces and sustains it all: the silent coming of God. This *can* happen. But whether it really does, and where, is the unfathomable secret of God, and of man's fundamental freedom. But it can occur anywhere, in forms ever new, and does in fact occur, though we can never point with certitude to any particular evidence. The event exists, though always shrouded in the incurable ambivalence of all that is human. It may occur anywhere: in a comfortable bourgeois sickroom, where the sick man, still hoping against hope, in a final act of surrender allows death to take possession of him in the last dread solitude; in the mud-holes of a battlefield; in the ultimate honesty—and it does exist—of a man who thinks himself an atheist and yet keeps doggedly on along the road to the unknown, nameless God, praising him; in the stern practicality with which, full of silent unselfishness, a man tries to serve his fellows in a research laboratory; where a child opens his heart to God; where a man is smitten with compunction for a guilt that seems fathomless to his fellows; in the bliss of love and in the horror of despair, incomprehensibly accepted, in life and in death, in glory and banality, in things sacred and things profane. This mystery may occur anywhere, because everything originates in this self-communicating love of God, because it embraces even guilt, and because already it has, in Jesus Christ, brought forth the event of its triumphant historical manifestation. It is the indissoluble beginning of both God's victory and ours, the triumph that manifests itself in such ordinary, humble garb that anyone

24

can find the improbable courage to believe and hope that God's tremendous love occurs even in one's own appalling humdrum life, where nothing seems to happen but birth and death, and in between, amid emptiness, and the guilt no man is spared, a little longing and a little faithfulness.

In this world, then, of God, of Jesus Christ, and of incomprehensibility there is to be a community to bear witness to Jesus: to attest God's vouchsafing of himself to the world, and its inevitable victory. This community does not coincide with the community of God's children, for by the infinite power of God's historical gift of himself those children are found everywhere, in all ages, in a countless multitude of forms, in all colours. And conversely: in inextricable confusion on the threshing-floor of this community of witnesses the wheat and chaff of world history still lie unwinnowed. But what really happens in the depths of world history must be explicitly attested, find its historical manifestation, must be proclaimed and occur anew by that very proclamation. This must be because the ultimate truth and reality of this tremendous history not only exists in Christ but has also become manifest in him, has been definitively fixed in that manifestation. So this community of witnesses comes from Jesus for the salvation of *the world* (note merely for their own salvation), attests him, points back in faith to him, his death, and his resurrection, and forward in hope to the revealing of his victory.

This community must be the community that dares to declare aloud, in, and despite, all the wretched bourgeois narrow-mindedness that is part of its lot, that the dreary plain of our existence also has peaks soaring up into the eternal light of the infinite God, peaks we can all scale, and that the awful bottomless abysses will hide God-filled depths we have not sounded, even when we think we have

25

experienced everything and found it all absurd. Unequivocally and audibly the witness of this community, with its incomprehensible courage which dares contradict all of man's miserable experience, should shout out its invincible faith: God exists; God is love; love's victory is already won; all the streams of bitter tears that still flow through our land have dried up at the source; all darkness is but the darkest part of the night that heralds the dawn; life is worthwhile. This testimony is the *raison d'être* of the community called the Church, insofar as it is more than a mere part of the totality of humanity which God will never allow to escape from his love. Its true, ultimate nature, the real work that it is set, is not how to teach man a little respect for God, not how to wring a little decency and kindness from man's brutal selfishness, is not the law, but the Gospel that God triumphs by his own doing and victoriously lavishes himself on this humanity and its world—is witness to that most improbable of facts which is the only ultimate truth.

Now since this community always gives the same witness, she must herself be *one*, requires cohesion and order; since she points back to Jesus Christ and ahead to him, this unity, this cohesion, and this order must come from Jesus Christ; since she is the community of witness to God's eschatologically victorious vouchsafing of himself to the world, since the historical manifestation of this vouchsafing happened in Christ as a permanent promise and this age in which we live is the last aeon of history, the community herself cannot perish; her witness, even her unity and order, are subject to the victorious mercy in which God vouchsafes himself to the world. She is there, the community of this witness; she does her work and justifies her existence whether she be great or small, for she does not witness for herself but for the salvation of the world, which takes places both inside and outside her own circle; but neither can she exempt any man from the call to share in witnessing to God, his Christ, and the approaching kingdom of God; she must summon all men to effect and experience in themselves this salvation of the world by witnessing to it before the world. And she knows that should a man guiltily turn a deaf ear to this summons, he would also lose what he is meant to bear witness to. She also knows she is the community which proclaims God's salvation for others, for everybody: the salvation which is there for all and takes place in glory for all who do not culpably reject it. She knows she is the community that proclaims an absolute hope from which she may exclude no one. This community is called the Church.

TRUSTING IN MYSTERY

If we accept this thinking, loving, hoping existence in spite of all the hasty, impatient pains and protests on the surface of our life; if we do not confuse responsibility with banality; then we have already given ourselves to God, and opened ourselves to him. Many people do that, even when they think they do not know God (we always have to know him as the Inconceivable, otherwise we have confused him with something else, which is an error that the self-confessed believers fall into all too often), even when in silent respect they do not trust themselves to speak his name.

In that kind of accepted existence, which obediently entrusts itself to mystery, as that to which we are subject and not that to which we are subject, something happens that we call 'grace' in our Christian terminology. God is and remains mystery. But he is the profundity in which human existence is accepted. He is the nearness and not merely the distance. He is forgiveness and not merely judgment. He silently and unutterably answers and fulfils the eternal human question, the groundlessness of hope and the infinite requirements of love. And he does all that of himself.

He does so silently and in that ground of our being which only opens itself to us if we obediently allow ourselves to be encompassed by that mystery, without ever wishing to conquer and rule it.

INVISIBLE SIGNS

God my Father, you are the God of free favours, of grace freely given. You show your mercy to whomever you please, where and when you choose.

If it's true that your calling of men to a share in your own life is a completely free gift, then, as I well understand, this summons is not something given to every man along with his nature. Man finds you only where you choose to be found.

And as proof that your salvation is a gratuitous gift, every man's road to eternal life, even though it leads to your infinity which is everywhere, must still take the 'detour' through that definite human being who was born in Palestine under Emperor Augustus and died under the Governor, Pontius Pilate. We must take the 'indirect route' leading through your Son who became man. Your grace comes to us not in the 'always and everywhere' of your all-pervasive Spirit, but in the 'here and now' of Jesus Christ.

Your Holy Spirit blows where he will—where *he* will, not where I will. He is not simply always there, whenever and wherever a man want him to be. We must go to him, there where he chooses to give his grace. And that's why your salvation is bound up with your visible Church. That's why your grace comes to us in visible signs.

GOD'S WORD

The word of God and of his mercy in Jesus Christ is the only one that holds out, delivers, and delights always and everywhere, steadfast till our death, till eternity. God's word in Jesus Christ our Lord, commissioned and authorized by him, is the word the priest addresses to us. He comes to you with the old message that is ever young, saying: Receive us as the ambassadors of Christ. Exert your heart and mind by God's grace to hear God's word in these human words of ours, our struggling, lamentable words that often seem to have paled—the holy, blessed, mighty word that brings us God himself and his everlasting life. If you accept us on these terms with brotherly understanding and forbearance, always gazing through us at the Lord who sent us, then, dear brothers and sisters, our word will bring into your lives the consolation, the strength, the eternal life that is offered to you in God's word. And this word entrusted to the priest by holy mission can be spoken into the concrete situation of an individual human life with an ultimate authority, an ultimate power, an ultimate relevance, such that, in accordance with God's promise, what he has done for men now becomes present in that life in ultimate truth, deed, and power. Then this word is called the sacramental word. And to speak this very word is in a special way the duty of a priest. He says: I baptize thee in the name of the Father . . . He says: Your sins are forgiven you. Through the anointment of the holy word he makes us men who can be ready to receive God's eternal life by

29

passing through death. Divinely commissioned by Christ, after he has pronounced Christ's words at the Last Supper he distributes Christ's true body and true blood amongst us.

The efficacious sacramental word entrusted to the priest sustains all this. He is steward of the mysteries of God. When he speaks this word the personality of the priest sinks farthest into the background and the Christian experiences the directest contact with God. Then, in a sense, only Christ's word rings out through the priest, because there is simply nothing else that he can say but Christ's word. It seems to be the most ordinary word, the word most often repeated, but that means it is Christ's word and so as priests of Christ and his Church we would pass it on to you, day in, day out. We do not enlarge much on it; we keep saying the same thing all through our priestly life. But of all the words that it is given us to say, this is the blessedest and mightiest, the one that most humbles us and exalts God in our life. For if it falls into your ready hearts, then what Christ has done for you occurs afresh. You have, in a manner of speaking, met the Lord face to face, you have found him and his grace. And on such a day we priests in our turn can but humbly beg you: At least accept this word from us. We are entrusted with it through no merit of our own. No less than you, we must believe it and take it into our hearts so that we too may be saved. So Christ's word, spoken to us and to you in his holy sacraments, is your salvation and ours. As brothers together let us hear and receive this one word in Jesus Christ with his grace, his mercy, and eternal life.

LOVE AND LAW

We must be agrowing, always as it were absorbing infinities into ourselves because it is our business to remain open to God. For having given us himself in his *agape,* he belongs to us. And so our life, our being, is full of endless potentialities that we exploit only by degrees, step by step, piecemeal. If we keep enriching ourselves in this way, accumulating grace and blessing, ever more selfless and more faithful, absorbing God who gives himself to us, then we begin to see the kind of love we could give away to others, simply by giving away ourselves, still half-grown, still tentative, still imperfect though we are. At best, our achievements in this world remain so fragmentary, we are so pitifully imprisoned within oursleves. When we give to others it is usually from afar, to show them that we really do want to love our neighbour. And when we try to give from nearby, try to show with words, or sacrifice, or faithfulness, that we want to love one another, it all remains so elementary. Now perhaps we understand a little better what St Paul means when he says: This love is the surpassing fulfilment of the law. Where laws are nothing more than laws, they can only represent a kind of rough-and-ready justice, distinguishing what is mine and what is the other fellow's, showing the individual what concrete goods and services he owes his neighbour. But exact calculations and legality are superseded when love enters the picture, when man gives himself with all his divine infinity to his neighbour, or at least tries to start doing so. Then he is no longer a man accomplishing something or rendering a service; he does more than comply with an objective norm which is equally binding on us all; he is a man perfecting himself by being the unique creature he is meant to be, perfecting himself because God has given him his own divine self in a unique way. And because what is involved here is a person, unique and irreplaceable, a person who achieves and perfects himself by lovingly giving himself away to others, all mere legality is superabundantly fulfilled and left behind. Thus love is the fulfilling of the law and the bond of perfection, as Paul says—that which will not pass away. That is why Paul can actually say: such a man has not only kept the law but more than fulfilled it, has passed beyond it and arrived at what must be a man's destination. For if we truly love our neighbour in God—only in God are we able to give ourselves away to our neighbour—, we really need not trouble about anything else. Law, with its demands, its over-harsh requirements, lies behind us. We have entered upon the blessed freedom of God's love for us, of our love for God, of the love that by God's grace we have for our neighbour. Only when we have got that length—not by our own powers but by the grace of God—shall we have reached our fulfilment in God.

ULTIMATE MYSTERY

Our existence is embraced by an ineffable mystery whom we call God. We can exclude him from our day-to-day awareness by the concerns and activity of our daily lives; we can drown the all-pervading silence of this mystery. But he is there: as the one comprehensive, all-bearing ground of all reality; as the comprehensive question that remains when all individual answers have been given; as the goal to which we reach beyond all individual goals and all individual good things of life; as the future which lies beyond all individual goals and keeps our ceaseless restless striving in motion; as the ultimate guarantee that there is really a responsibility for our freedom which cannot be shifted on to someone else, which we cannot elude by leaping into nothingness; as the one truth in which all individual knowledge has its ultimate home and order; as the promise that selfless love will not be disappointed.

This ultimate mystery at the root of reality and of our lives is nameless, impenetrable, something we cannot dominate with our concepts and life calculations, something that gives itself only when we yield to it in worship. We call it God. But this 'name' is only a reminder of the nameless and the incomprehensible, of the bright abyss to which our life tends, either to perish in it for ever or to find its definitive fulfilment. Every science, even the most up-to-date and advanced, deals with individual things and establishes connexions among them in order to be able to control them in the service of life. No science, however, can dominate the one mystery which embraces everything and which in all partial knowledge becomes only the more incomprehensible and burning; either all sciences flee it in doubt and confusion, or they must rise in man to the worship of the fundamental mystery of all reality and all life.

When the sciences reach their limits (which can be experienced even when an unlimited land of investigable matter still lies stretched out before them), either they leave man resigned, alone with his question about the unity and totality of his world and reality, or they try—and in the end fatally—to explain the ultimate questions away as meaningless and unanswerable, or they appeal in sceptical despair to nothingness, which contains no answer. We who believe, however, do not flee this ultimate mystery, we enter into it, we know that this abyss is the only ground on which in the final analysis we can build. We appeal to this mystery; we make it the centre of our lives, the goal to which all the roads of our history lead, even though and precisely because they lead into the incomprehensible.

We call this mystery God, and when we confess our belief in God, we know that in our lives, at the heart of our lives, we have to do business with this God, to experience always the inexpressibility of his mystery, because we are always the questioners who can never definitively arrive there, because we are and remain in everything in our lives, right up to the last question which is death, the ones about whom we are asking questions.

FAITH

In its real and living core, this Christian faith is not a complicated mass of difficult and obscure propositions the content of which is foreign to the actual experiences of our lives, but something extremely simple which, once we have really grasped and experienced it, cannot be separated from, or conceived apart from, our lives. This simple faith can then be broken down into a mutiplicity of single dogmas, but only if this multiplicity of doctrines is constantly referred back to, and understood to derive from, that simple living core, can the individual dogmas, insofar as they expressly engage us in our religious life as a whole (which *a priori* is not necessarily the case), become intelligible to us today.

We cannot escape the difficulty of accepting and 'realizing' this multiplicity of dogmas today just by appealing to the fact that the revelation of the dogmas was known before their content, because even the fact of this revelation cannot really be effectively substantiated today unless we also argue from the content of what is revealed. In what, does this simple and living core of the Christian faith, which still makes belief possible indeed easy for us today, consist?

This question can evidently be answered in a variety of

ways and with a variety of different formulations, even though these various answers ultimately mean the same things. With this reservation I shall attempt to outline a single answer here. It is in three intimately connected and mutually conditioned parts: *we who believe* know that we are ineluctably engaged by the incomprehensible mystery of our lives whom we call God, and who ceaselessly and silently grasps us and challenges our hope and love even when we show little concern for him in the practice of our lives or even actually deny him in theory; *we who believe* are convinced that this incomprehensible mystery whom we call God has definitively and forgivingly promised himself to us in the life, death and eternal living presence of Jesus of Nazareth, as the content and eternal validity of our own lives, which do not perish. *We who believe* constitute, in this confession of God in Jesus Christ, the community of believers, the Church, which attests this message of God in Jesus Christ to the whole world for its salvation. I shall pause a little at each of the three fundamental statements of the faith so that we can appreciate more easily that our faith still meets the needs of our human situation today and is still credible.

QUESTION AND ANSWER

We believe in Jesus the Christ, that is, in God's self-promise in forgiveness and eternal life which has been persuasively announced in his life. No one forces us to accept in faith God's answer, who is Jesus crucified and risen. But also no one can convince us that there is another, better and more comprehensive answer to the question ineluctably and inexorably posed by our own life, even when we try to ignore this question. No one will persuade us that we have not heard the question. Once we pose it and face up to it, we find it easy to believe that in Jesus we have heard an answer to it.

This answer does not answer all the thousand and one questions of a particular kind which our life poses, but it contains all these individual answered or unanswered questions in the saving mystery of God. All these questions of life ultimately come together in the one question which death poses in our life. But we have the courage of believing hope to fall with Jesus' death into the abyss of God as into our own definitiveness, our home and our eternal life. Because we can confidently die only with him, and because we still die with him when, even without knowing him explicitly, we surrender in calm hope to the mystery of life, we can here and now live this life in confidence with him even though it still stands under the mystery of death.

FORERUNNERS

We are all pilgrims on the wearisome roads of our life. There is always something ahead of us that we have not yet overtaken. When we do catch up with something it immediately becomes an injunction to leave it behind us and to go onwards. Every end becomes a beginning. There is no resting place or abiding city. Every answer is a new question. Every good fortune is a new longing. Every victory is only the beginning of a defeat.

Surely we are forerunners? As parents we are the forerunners of our children. As old people, the forerunners of the young. As the scientists and scholars of today, the forerunners of those of tomorrow. As the politicians of today, the forerunners of those to come, who will scatter and suppress those of today.

We so quickly change the goals, words, and obvious characteristics of our projects, of politics, of the sciences, and of art. Every man seems to march into his present moment with the feeling that now the real thing is coming, the truly valid thing that is once and for all, only then—very soon, alas!—to perceive that his present is turning into past; that he is old-fashioned and out-of-date; that he no longer understands and is no longer understood.

Aren't we always despatching messengers from the dungeon of our compulsions and disappointments? We send them to find the real thing, that which is ultimately valid, even though we do not really know where to direct these messengers of our unassuaged longing?

Isn't death, which swallows us all, the only thing that we are sure to catch up with on our way? In our strange confusion we try to hold back the fleeting moment and to get to the next moment ahead more quickly than ever it could get to us. We who on all human pathways are always forerunners of the transient are always tempted to elevate our plans and projects to the level of something that is to come, an ultimate that will remain for ever. It seems that something of the idiocy which makes a man see everything and everyone else as transitory and himself as ultimate, and refuse to be a mere forerunner of an incalculable future, is an almost inevitable feature of the world on its way.

We are no more than predecessors. The goal of our journeying seems always to remain far ahead of us, to stay beyond our power and always to fade into new perspectives of distance, even when we think we are approaching it.

EXPLAINING THE TRINITY

The words 'person' and 'essence' only tell us in another form the same thing that we already know from original experience and the statement of faith. We are told that we are dealing with God in his radical incomprehensible Godhead (Father), that this Godhead is really given to us in the Son and the Holy Spirit; yet that we are not to consider them as created intermediaries of this Godhead, nor merely as other words for the Godhead of the Father, who is with us through them. The historical origin of these concepts and the context in which they originated do not tell us whether they contain or may contain not only a logical, but also an ontic explanation.

By a *logical* explanation of a statement about a certain state of affairs, I mean an explanation which makes the statement in question clear, that is, more precise, less liable to be misunderstood. A logical explanation clarifies the statement independently of anything else. To put it roughly: the logical explanation explains by making more precise; it does not use one state of affairs to explain another one. Hence all the concepts used to explain that statement can be derived from it. This would still be the case if the *verbal* terminology used in the explanation were obtained elsewhere, provided only that it be well understood (explicitly or implicitly) that the employed terminology is meant only within the sense and scope of what is being explained.

An *ontic* explanation is one that takes into account *another* state of affairs, in such a way that this helps us to avoid misunderstandings by listing the cause of something, the exact and concrete way in which something comes about. Thus when everything turns dark before my eyes, I can ontically explain this fact by attributing it to a turning-off of the light, or to the physiological atrophy of my optic nerve.

It follows at once that a logical explanation can be understood only if it refers always to the statement which is to be explained. The ontic explanation, on the other hand (as is clear from our simple example), is not based on anything that needs explaining; it stands of itself, since it takes another state of affairs into account. Yet, though the logical explanation refers continually back to the statement in need of explanation, and although it lives from this reference and turns into empty verbalism and conceptual rationalism without it, it is and remains a very important kind of explanation. We cannot show here why this is the case. Everyone knows this at heart and makes use of such explanations.

He who does biblical theology wishes to say exactly what the Scripture says, yet he cannot simply repeat the words of Scripture. In this respect, it seems to me, the only but essential difference between Protestant and Catholic theology is this: that for the Catholic theologian the logical explanation of the words of Scripture by the Church can definitely become a statement of faith; whereas for the Protestant theologian it remains basically theology, and it may always be revised and reversed. Let us add this, however: that although a logical explanation can become for us an unchangeable dogma, we see that even then it differs qualitatively from Scripture. Furthermore, not only insofar as it validly binds our faith, but also for its meaning and interpretation, such a formula always looks back to te the words of Scripture (or of the original tradition). It is also true that this word of Scripture remains alive and normative only if, through a dogmatically binding (logical) explanation, it abides in the ever-changing historical situation.

YOU ARE IN PROCESS

Slowly a light is beginning to dawn. I'm beginning to understand something I have known for a long time: You are still in the process of your coming. Your appearance in the form of a slave was only the beginning of your coming, a beginning in which you chose to redeem men by embracing the very slavery from which you were freeing them. And *you* can really achieve yor purpose in this paradoxical way, because the paths that *you* tread have a real ending, the narrow passes which *you* enter soon open out into broad liberty, the cross that *you* carry inevitably becomes a brilliant banner of triumph.

Actually you haven't come—you're still coming. From your incarnation to the end of this era is only an instant, even though millennia may elapse and, being blessed by you, pass on to become a small part of this instant. It is all only the one, single moment of your single act, which catches up our destiny into your own human life, and sweeps us along to our eternal home in the broad expanses of your divine life.

Since you have already begun this definitive deed, your final action in this creation, nothing new can really happen any more. Our present era is the last: in the deepest roots of all things, time is already standing still. 'The final age of the world has come upon us' (1 Cor 10.11). There is only a single period left in this world: your Advent. And when this last day comes to a close, then there will be no more time, but only you in your eternity.

If deeds measure time, and not time deeds—if one new event ushers in a new age, then a new age, and indeed the last, has dawned with your incarnation. For what could still happen, that this age does not already carry in its womb? That we should become partakers of your being? But that has already happened, the moment you deigned to become partaker of our humanity.

It is said that you will come again, and this is true. But the word *again* is misleading. It won't really be 'another' coming, because you have never really gone away. In the human existence which you made your own for all eternity, you have never left us.

But still you will come again, because the fact that you have already come must continue to be revealed ever more clearly. It will become progressively more manifest to the world that the heart of all things is already transformed, because you have taken them all to your heart.

You must continue to come more and more. What has already taken place in the roots of all reality must be made more and more apparent. The false appearance of our world, the shabby pretence that it has not been liberated from finiteness through your assuming finiteness into your own life, must be more and more thoroughly rooted out and destroyed.

Behold, you come. And your coming is neither past nor future, but the present, which has only to reach its fulfilment. Now it is still the one single hour of your advent, at the end of which we too shall have found out that you have really come.

God who is to come, grant me the grace to live now, in the hour of your advent, in such a way that I may merit to live in you forever, in the blissful hour of your eternity.

SHINING

If we are persevering in faith, if we are the children of God and hence the children of his eternal election, then we should always pray with the hope that the days of darkness will be shortened. And always, whether we live or die, we must shine like stars in heaven. That is our duty, to act in the sight of God in heaven and of our historical age on earth in the way the Lord has told us to act: in sobriety and resolution, in prayer and in the awareness that we are the elect for whose sake the blessing and the promise have been given.

CHRISTIANITY

The pre-history of Christianity must comprise all history back to its very origins, even if this for technical reasons is omitted in practice in the writing of church history. Since the history of Christianity is the history of the dialogue between God and man, it has its own centre and real beginning (as opposed to its pre-history) in the absolute and enduring intimacy of the dialogue between God and humanity in Jesus Christ, in whom word and answer of that dialogue are one person. On the other hand, since the dialogue takes place, as human dialogue, by affirmation and denial, it always involves the other partner outside (mankind called by God) and the refusal and failure within (Christians themselves). In this connexion it is to be noted that the Church's own genuine theological and historical conception of itself as the society which must understand itself on the basis of the promised future, must be formed on the basis of that future. Theological Church history must look into the future in order to be able correctly to perceive the past. Otherwise it inevitably becomes simply a part of the general history of the world and of religions.

FREE LOVE OF GOD

When freedom is seen as the free love of God in dialogue with the partner necessary to such freely given love, it appears as the essential dignity of the person. This view of freedom must be the foundation of the doctrine of a rightly understood freedom of conscience and of the right of freedom to room for is concrete realization in face of undue restrictions laid upon it by State or Church.

In such a concept of freedom, it would be seen to be in need of interpretation by God. It cannot 'judge itself' because it is historical and hence while its process is still going on it can never be fully present to reflection. This interpretation by God must be seen as a verdict of guilty and a verdict of gracious acquittal passed upon guilty freedom. It will then be seen that the freedom of choice (of the Greek notion) stands in the same relation to Christian freedom, by reason of the liberating grace of God, as nature stands to grace. The former, while retaining its nature, is still frustrated of its true sense where it is not elevated and redeemed by the freedom of the children of God.

Hence the proper attitude of man to his freedom must be defined as thankfulness. It is a welcome gift which he gladly accepts, not something to which he is 'condemned'. And because his individual deeds and basic choice are in principle not amenable to full and certain cognizance, it is only by hoping in God that he can accept it without being plagued by scruples or threatened with self-righteousness.

Hence in theology freedom is understood as having its source and goal in God (who is its 'object' and the 'horizon' of all possible objects). In this way it is total dominion over the self, aiming at the definitive. It is self-mastery bestowed on man in the dialogue with God, where he is called to the finality of love's decision. Freedom always finds itself fettered in an irremediable situation of disaster and as it accepts this verdict in faith, always finds itself the recipient of liberty through Jesus Christ. But in this way—at a level on which the systematic theology of freedom must cancel itself out by finding itself safely on a higher plane—freedom is a mystery to itself and all others. It is mystery as the primordial dialogue, as freedom liberated from bondage and called into the absolute mystery.

MAN

Man is an individual personal subject with a unique history of freedom for which no one else can deputize, and at the same time a social being who can only have a history in the unity of the one humanity. He is never merely a numerical 'case' of the collectivity, and he is never so much an individual that he could be himself without inter-communication with his fellows, without his 'world'. Both aspects bear upon each other. Inter-communication and self-realization, self-possession, grow in principle in like and not inverse proportion. Man's social orientation, taken in its totality, is not 'subsidiary' in relation to the uniqueness of the individual free person but equally primordial and essential to it. And the social nature of man is again multi-dimensional: personal inter-communication (fellowship) in love, communication in the same truth and common cultural values and acquisitions, institutionalized society, biological and economic interdependence and so on. A single such dimension may no doubt be considered as subsidiary with regard to the human person as a whole. Antagonisms and conflicts occur between the various dimensions, and 'levels' of man as 'individual' and between individual men (and so too with humanity, people, society, group and State). Their concrete

44

mutual relationship is one of perpetual historical change.

So too man is a sexual being. His sexuality should not be assumed from the start to be a individual faculty, that of generation in this case. It is a quality which affects all the individual determinations of man, in a different way in each case. Hence it too exists on many levels and shares in the historicity of man and his 'indefinability', as a spiritual being whose historical self-interpretation makes up his concrete essence but loses itself constantly in the mystery of God.

The origin and goal of man's existence is the self-communication of God. This free self-communication of God, when consistently thought out in relation to the nature of historical man, has its own history. Hence it must reach a phase of victorious irreversibility, and has in fact reached in it in Jesus Christ. Hence it aims from the start at this point as its final cause, and so this self-communication is always (even in the supralapsarian order) Christological. Man was always willed as member of a humanity and sharer of a human history which attain their most proper structure and real hope of the future in the incarnation of the divine Logos, the eschatological climax of the divine self-communication.

The divine self-communication, as the free history of God himself, is also the ultimate ground and content of the history of man's freedom, in acceptance of rejection. But this is so only in the sense that while the outcome of the history of salvation of the individual remains open, the positive outcome of the collective history of man's salvation in Jesus Christ is already assured. Man as such, mankind in its history, moves within the historical reality, already made manifest, of the absolute salvific will of God. The real self-alienation of man, who is only in possession of himself when attained victoriously by the self-communication of

God which brings about the positive Yes of his freedom, has been fundamentally overcome since Jesus Christ. The individual's hope is assured when he inserts it into the sure hope of mankind which is definitively triumphant in Christ.

LOVE THE EARTH

Christ is already in the midst of the poor things of this earth—the earth which we cannot leave because she is our mother. He is in the ineffable yearning of all creatures who, without knowing it, yearn for a share in the transfiguration of his body. He is in the history of the earth, whose blind course, with all its victories and all its crashing defeats, steers with uncanny precision towards the day when his splendour, transforming everything, will erupt out of the earth's own depths. He is in all the tears as hidden joy, and in every death as the life that conquers by seeming to die. He is in the beggar, to whom we give a coin, as the secret rich reward that returns to the giver. He is in the miserable defeats of his servants as the victory that belongs to God alone. He is in our weakness as the strength that dares to let itself seem weak, because it is invincible. He himself is even right in the midst of sin as the mercy of everlasting life that is prepared to be patient to the end. He is present as the mysterious law and the innermost essence of all things— the law that triumphs and succeeds even when all order seems to be crumbling. He is with us like the light and air of day, which we do not notice; like the mysterious law of a motion that we do not grasp, because the segment of this motion that we ourselves experience is too short for a formula to be educed by us. But he is there. He is the heart of this earthly world and the mysterious seal of its eternal validity.

That is why we children of the earth may love the earth; that is why we must love her, even when she terrifies us and makes us tremble with her misery and her destiny of death. For ever since Christ, through his death and resurrection, penetrated the earth for all time, her misery has become provisional and a mere test of our faith.

BECOMING

If the creation of the soul by God is regarded as a case, even if a distinctive case, of becoming through self-transcendence, it loses its appearance of being miraculous and predicamental. This creation becomes an instance of God's operation as it is always to be though of. The divine activity is not really predicamental. It does not cause something which the creature does not cause, for it does not cause side by side with the activity of the creature. It causes the operation of the creature which exceeds and transcends its own possibilities. And this is the situation in which a creature always is; it belongs to its essence. The transcendental character of God's operation in relation to the world must never in any respect be thought of as a purely static support of the world. The divine transcendent function as ground of the world posits the world as a world in movement, involved in becoming by rising above and beyond, and these ascents necessarily occur at points of time in the history of this developing world. But the fact that God makes possible such self-transcendence by finite causes does not mean that God's action thereby occupies a definite point in time or involves a predicamental miraculous intervention in the world.

GOD'S TRUTH

God's truth is ever one and the same, definitive. It is proclaimed by the Church's magisterium. When and where that magisterium has expressed the truth entrusted to her by Christ in a form that binds the conscience of the faithful, that truth in that form is true and valid for all time. Theology and preaching will always refer back to such formularies of revealed truth drawn up in the course of the Church's history, secure in the knowledge that the truth meant was, in fact, rightly expressed in them. And this despite the fact that no formulation of the truths of faith in human words is ever adequate to the object referred to by them, and that at least in principle, any of them could be replaced by an even better, more comprehensive one. An intellectual, conceptual formulary is never merely the subsequent reflection of an experience of faith in itself irrational, as the modernist misconception of the intellectual element in faith would have it. But God's truth in human words is not, for all that, given merely in order to wander through the text books of dogmatic theology in printed propositions perpetually monotonous. It is intended rather for a vital encounter with the actual concrete individual, to penetrate into his mind and heart, become his very flesh and blood, bring him into the truth. That calls for a ceaselessly renewed assimilation by the individual. Just as he is, in his age, with his experiences, his lot, his intellectual situation, which is not only that of ecclesiastical Christianity but also that of the age generally, the individual must hear God's message ever anew, in all his own individuality. And since not the audible message, but only the message actually heard can be believed by a human being, and as the truth of revelation does not consist in a mere timeless intrinsic validity, but can only and is only intended

48

to have an earthly existence by being actually believed in fact, the pure and ever identical truth of the gospel must bear the stamp of the age in the actual concrete accomplishment of being known and acknowledged in each successive epoch.

CHANGE AND HISTORY

The real coming into being of what is higher through the effective self-transcendence of an inferior cause, *and* enduring creation from above, are simply two sides, equally true and real, of the one marvel of change and history. This is seen to be the highest instance of the principle that God in his relation of freedom to his creation is, after all, not a finite cause side by side with others in the world, but is the living, permanent transcendent ground of the self-government of the world itself. It is precisely this principle which also applies *suo modo* to the relation between God and man in the occurrence and history of revelation; in fact it applies here in the highest degree, because this history must in the highest degree be both the act of God and of man, if it is to constitute the highest reality in the being and becoming of the world. If it is possible in principle to overcome in that way the sterile antithesis of immanentism and extrinsicism in the ontological interpretation of change and history in general, then theology must also surmount such an antithesis in the question which concerns us here.

FREE ACCEPTANCE

The car in which we ride through life may seem to us a fine, comfortable caravan which takes us on a holiday trip through beautiful scenery. But it is also the prison van of our finite being, in which we are shut up with our disappointments and the misery of our boring daily life, in which we ride on to our final end, which is death. We all are cross-bearers in the sober sense which we have discussed above. No one can rid himself of this cross of existence. But precisely for this reason it is difficult to know whether we accept this cross in faith, hope and love to our salvation, or whether we only bear it protesting secretly, because we cannot free ourselves from it but are nailed to it like the robber on the left of Jesus, who cursed his fate and blasphemed the crucified Lord by his side. It is almost impossible to distinguish and decide between these two attitudes. And yet all depends on this distinction. Everything—that is the meaning which we give to our life or rather which we allow God to give it, and thus our salvation. The one question is whether we accept it or not. When do we accept it? Certainly not if we talk much about it and imagine ourselves very brave. Certainly not by exaggerating the little sorrows of our daily life and whining and whimpering about them. Certainly not if we imagine that the will to bear the cross prevents us from defending ourselves and from leading a free, healthy and sound life as long as is at all possible. Nor does the word of the cross allow us to be indifferent to the cross of another and only interested in our own comfort. But to accept the cross does not mean either that we should take a perverse pleasure in pain or be so dulled that we no longer feel it. But in what, then, does this acceptance consist? It is difficult to say, because it can take so many forms that a common factor is scarcely noticeable. It may appear as a brave will to fight on, as sober patience, a heroic love of the cross, uncomplaining sharing in the fate of others, self-forgetfulness in the sorrows of one's neighbour and in many other forms. It seems to me that the crucified Lord has fathomed all these forms when he cried out on the cross: My God, my God, why hast thou forsaken me! and when he prayed: Father, into thy hands I commend my life. In the first quotation the cross remains incomprehensible and is not explained away, while in the second it is accepted as this remaining mystery. Both together constitute the truth of the acceptance. The whole may be present even if we only utter the first cry while the second is there, though it remains unspoken. Whether or not we become wholly dumb when death takes away our voice, that is perhaps the last mystery of our life.

TRAINING FOR LOVE

Today a training for freedom is necessarily a training for love which patiently accepts those restrictions without which the many who are to be loved can no longer exist today. Where stubborn rebellion is not simply the instinctive reaction of a caged animal fettered by social ties, it may often be something like the almost inevitable practice of freedom, the subject's acceptance of its own responsibility. Such rebellion may also be the liberation from the unjust restrictions which an ancient society with fossilized traditions has fashioned for itself. Nevertheless, rebellion is not the last word of freedom, it is not its most mature form, especially not if it is in the deepest sense unsocial, hence both old-fashioned and loveless.

GLORY

Man likes to give half-answers. He likes to escape to where he does not have to make a clear decision. That is understandable. We are travellers and consequently in a condition in which everything, meaning and meaninglessness, death and life, is still mixed together, half finished, incomplete. But it cannot remain so. It is moving on. And the end cannot be other than clear and plain. Consequently reality compels us, whether we wish or not, to give a plain answer in our own lives. And so the question is put to us: Death or life? Meaning or meaninglessness? Ideals which are nebulously inconclusive or real facts? If by faith and action we plainly decide for meaning and life as facts, and consider life and death as mere *ideals* to be inadequate, if we affirm life and meaning as a fact, not half-heartedly but whole-heartedly in endless magnitude and scope, then whether we know it or not we have said Easter. And we Christians know this. We know that the reality of Easter is not simply the essence hidden in the depth of our life but is the truth and reality of our faith called by its name and explicitly professed. And so we comprise the whole history of nature and of mankind in a celebration which in rite contains the actual reality celebrated, and we make the ultimate statement about it: I believe in the resurrection of the body (flesh) and life everlasting. I believe that the beginning of the glory of all things has already come upon us, that we, apparently so lost, wandering and seeking far away, are already encompassed by infinite blessedness. For the end has already begun. And it is glory.

OPENNESS OF HEART

Whenever a human being in real personal freedom opens his heart to his neighbour, he has already by that very fact done more than simply loved that neighbour, because all that was already encompassed by the grace of God. He has loved his neighbour and in his neighbour he has already loved God. Because he cannot meet his neighbour with love except through the fact that the dynamism of his spiritual freedom supported by the grace of God is already itself always a dynamism towards the unutterable holy mystery which we call God.

CELEBRATION

Our heart is weak and cowardly and always overtaxed by what the word of God demands of us. That word must give us what it requires of us. That is why we celebrate the Lord's Supper. We announce his death which redeems us into the freedom of the children of God. We place ourselves under the law of his cross, on which ultimate human powerlessness, obediently in agreement with itself, became an act manifesting the power of God. We receive the Body of the Lord which was given for us, so that each who receives it with faith may not be left alone with his weakness any more, so that in him too the kindness of the living God may be effective and grant him to begin the everyday practice of obvious commonplace duty. In this everyday duty, provided it is accepted quite unconditionally, death is present in an inner way that can easily be overlooked. For there is unrewarded sacrifice there, absolutely silent renunciation, the hazardous enterprise that demands all and apparently gives nothing. There, in other words, is death, renunciation, silent acceptance. A person to whom it is given to do and suffer this, from a source which he does not know, dies with Christ whether he knows it or not. Because we know this in faith, we celebrate the Lord's Supper, in which he himself accepted his death. It is a terrible thing to place oneself under the cross of him who expressed the ultimate when he commended his life into the hands of him whom he called the God who had forsaken him. But there alone is the burning bush of redemption and love.

HOLY ORIGIN

Ultimately only the man who believes in the holy origin can believe in a final salvation, only he can believe in an infinite future (for all else would merely be transitory and a beginning of death) for whom history starts with this infinite future that posits the beginning of history. Only if a man believes in a holy God will he believe in a blessed life to come. Only few dare to say that they regard such a future as a chimera. And these few protest against the absurdity of existence probably only because they, too, measure life by the standard that belongs to eternal life and which they, too, presuppose. Hence all might confess: I believe in God, the almighty Father. Though even then there would still be the problems which are bitter until the bitterness of death. But they would be mysteriously redeemed.

LOVE

The encounter with the neighbour in love must be recognized not as one experience among others, but as the central act of human existence which integrates the whole personal content of experience. Finally, any absolute, (positive) moral decision must be recognized as implicit theism and 'anonymous Christianity'. Under these circumstances, it can be affirmed on principle that the act by which the neighbour is loved *is* really the primal (though still non-explicit) act by which God is loved.

PROPHECY

Prophecy, according to 1 Corinthians 13.9, is a mere fragment in comparison to charity, which alone has the strength to embrace even the perpetual darkness of the future, which no prophecy could so illumine as to banish all dangers from it. For love alone can accept such a future from the hands of God as a gift of his wisdom and his love. There will ever be true and false prophets in the kingdom of Christ. So the exhortation is always opportune: 'extinguish not the spirit; despise not prophecies; but prove all things; hold fast that which is good' (1 Thess. 5.19-21). The good in every prophecy is ultimately shown if it awakens us to the gravity of decision in courageous faith, if it makes clear to us that the world is in a deplorable state (which we never like to admit), if it steels our patience and fortifies our faith that God has already triumphed, even if in this world we still have distress, if it fills us with confidence in the one Lord of the still secret future, if it brings us to prayer, to conversion of heart, and to faith that nothing shall separate us from the love of Christ.

HIDDEN IN GOD

Our beginning is hidden in God. It is decided. Only when we have arrived will we fully know what our origin is. For God is mystery as such, and what he posited when he established us in our beginning is still the mystery of his free will hidden in his revealed word. But without evacuating the mystery, we can say that there belongs to our beginning the earth which God has created, the ancestors whose history God ruled with wisdom and mercy, Jesus Christ, the Church and baptism, earth and eternity. All is there, everything whatsoever which exists is silently concentrated

55

in the well-spring of our own existence and all the rest is pervaded by what each in himself and therefore as a beginning posited by God uniquely and unrepeatedly is. With what is hard and what is easy, delicate and harsh, with what belongs to the abyss and what is heavenly. All is encompassed by God, his knowledge and his love. All has to be accepted. And we advance towards it all; we experience everything, one thing after another, until future and origin coincide. One thing about this beginning, however, has already been said to us by the word of God. The possibility of acceptance itself belongs to the might of the divinely posited beginning. And if we accept, we have accepted sheer love and happiness. For even if in our beginning the difference between God's will and human will is interposed, even if even in the beginning our lot is decided both by God *and* by the history of guilt, nevertheless precisely in our case even this contradiction is always merely permitted and is already encompassed by pure love and forgiveness. And the more that love and forgiveness which encompasses and belongs to our beginning is accepted in the pain of life and in the death which gives life, and the more this original element emerges and is allowed to manifest itself and pervade our history, the more the difference, the contradiction in the beginning is resolved and redeemed. And all the more will it be revealed that we ourselves were also implied in that pure beginning whose feast day we are celebrating. When the beginning has found itself in the fulfilment and has been fulfilled in the freedom of accepting love, *God* will be all in all. Because then all will belong to all, the differences will of course still be there but they will have been transformed and will belong to the blessedness of unifying love, and no longer to separation. And for that reason this feast is *our* feast. For it is the feast of the freely bestowed love in which all of us are comprised, each in his place and rank.

ETERNAL LIFE

Whoever stands before the graves of Auschwitz or Bangladesh or other monuments to the absurdity of human life and manages neither to run away (because he cannot tolerate this absurdity) nor to fall into cynical doubt, believes in what we Christians call eternal life, even though his mind does not grasp it, and whether he can tolerate this statement of radical courage or not. One can live radical love, loyalty and responsibility which can never in the long run 'pay' *and* 'think' that all human life ends in the empty meaningless void, but in the very act of such a life the thought is belied, and it is contradicted by one's deeds.

AUTHENTIC VISION

An authentic vision may probably be explained as a purely spiritual touch of God affecting the innermost centre of a man and spreading from there to all his faculties, his thought and imagination, which transform this touch. Hence, when a 'vision' reaches the consciousness of the visionary it has already passed through the medium of his subjectivity, and therefore *also* bears his individual characteristics as regards language, interests, theological presuppositions and so forth. Hence the authentic vision is both divine and human, and because it is also human it is also affected by the visionary's nationality and the time in which he lives. In fact nothing else could be expected. It may well be assumed that in the case of a divinely caused vision of a heavenly person, too, though he or she appears to be there in the body, we have nevertheless to do with an imaginary vision, that means it is seen within the sphere of the interior imagination. This does not exclude that this vision is caused by an actual divine touch of the centre of the person (not merely by the visionary's own imagination) and that this touch is correctly translated into an imaginary picture. But Catholic theology does not offer an unanimous and binding opinion on this subject.

PRIVATE REVELATION

The possibility of private revelation through visions and associated auditory experiences is evident in principle for a Christian. God as a free personal being can make himself perceptible to the created spirit, not only through his works but also by his free, personal word. And he can do it in such a manner that this communication of God is not simply himself in the direct vision of the Godhead, or in the dimension of a blessed intellect emptied of all that is finite, but also, and for a Christian who believes in God's incarnation this is essential, in such a way that this communication is bound up with a particular place and time, with a concrete word or command, with a finite reality or truth, and so that it occurs with, or is connected with the 'apparition' of an object presented to the internal or external senses, which object represents and manifests God, his will, or the like.

GOD LOVES MAN

Ultimately, God's *agape* consists in his giving himself in love to the world in the spiritual creature. Through his self-communication he makes himself the inmost mystery of his creation, and its history and its fulfilment. He is not just Lord and Guardian, while creation itself remains 'outside' God. This love is the cause of there being others than itself, but it holds these differences together in their relationship to its own oneness, which is God. It contains

58

(analogously) an element of 'jealousy' ('desire') because the self-sufficient God willed in a free act of love to need a world which is his own history because of his self-communication in grace and the incarnation. It is dialogical ('bridal'), because it is the foundation and principle of man's love for God, since by grace man can love God in a divine way, just as he can utter the word *of God* in human words. In this way man's loving Yes to God is from God. This explains why the notion of 'Father' is only partially adequate to express the love of God for man. 'Son' must be understood in the sense in which Jesus knew himself to be Son and us as sons by participation. It is only the radical intimacy of self-communication in grace and the incarnation that eliminates the overtones of the external and paternalistic which may be heard in the 'Fatherliness' of God. This love can appear as the sovereign law which demands the humbly obedient love of the 'servant'. But then all the elements which go to make up the relationship of law and gospel must be considered.

It is difficult to preach today that God loves man, that by his self-communication he is love itself for him. This situation must be seen clearly and soberly. It has become clearer—though it was 'always' recognized—that God is not part of the world, that he is not to be found as a particular reality within the realm of our experience. His 'distance', his inexpressibility, the radical mysteriousness of his being, is the epochal hall-mark imposed on our existence. It is not so easy to realize as is sometimes supposed in unthinking pious talk that this God can love us, with a personal relationship to each individual which offers shelter to each. The atheism which appears as 'silence about that of which one cannot clearly speak', as well as the atheism of tragic despair at the horrors of human existence, are now challenges which consistently menace even the faith of

Christian theists in the love of God, in a loving God. We cannot now speak of God's love for us as though we were addressing men who have repressed all their experiences of the absurd and are so comfortably well-balanced that they find it very instructive to be told that the world is on the whole very well ordered and governed by a God of love. There must be a deep solidarity with a world in torment before one dares speak of the love of God. And then all merely 'philosophical' analysis will naturally fall away. To speak of the love of God will be to testify to it in deeds and words, to appeal to men for an ultimate decision in faith and love, where no stringent assurance can be provided. After Auschwitz, it has been said, there is nothing for it but to be an atheist. But it has also been said of the dead of Auschwitz that in fact we have to believe in God and hope in his love, since there is no justification for them otherwise and they are betrayed by their own absurdity. In any case, it has to be clearly affirmed that the happiness of posterity—always hoped and planned for in the world and just as constantly crashing to ruin—does not justify the miseries of the past and present. We must not flinch from asserting the hard truth that the love of God is just as much of a mystery as God himself. Cursing the darkness of the world does not make it any brighter. To bear the predestined impotence of our faith in God's love is not the same as to refuse culpably to believe in that love, though frustration and unbelief may not be very far apart. And to love others truly, in deed and will, without self-deception, to do so as an absolutely sacred duty, is fundamentally to believe in God and his love for man, even perhaps unknown to oneself.

FOR ALL MEN

Some people who reject the orthodox formulas of Christology (because they mistake their meaning) may nevertheless in fact actually exercise genuine faith in the incarnation of the Word of God. If in view of Jesus' cross and death, someone really believes that the living God has uttered in Jesus his ultimate, decisive, irrevocable and comprehensive Word and so has delivered man from all the bondage and tyranny which are among the existentials of his imprisoned, guilty, deathward-bound existence, then he believes something which is only true and real if Jesus is he whom the faith of Christendom professes. Such people believe in the incarnation of the Word of God whether they explicitly realize this or not. That is not to deny the importance of an objectively correct formulary which is the ecclesiastical and sociological basis of common thought and belief. But only a heretic who equates the circle of those who really believe the saving truth in the depth of their heart with the circle of those who profess the orthodox formulas of the Church (the Catholic cannot do that) can deny *a priori* that someone can believe in Jesus Christ even though he rejects the correct Christological formula. In the living of human life, it is not possible existentially to adopt just any position, however theoretically conceivable. Consequently anyone who does allow Jesus to convey to him the ultimate truth about his life, and professes that in him and in his death God conveys the ultimate truth in view of which he lives and dies, by that very fact accepts Jesus as the Son of God whom the Church confesses. And that is so, however he himself expresses that active faith practised in his life, even if theoretically it is an unsuccessful formula, or even conceptually false.

It is possible to go even further. Some encounter Jesus

Christ yet do not realize that they are coming into contact with someone into whose life and death they are plunging as their destiny. Created freedom always involves the risk of what has been overlooked, what is inwardly hidden in what is seen and willed, whether that is realized or not. It is true that what is absolutely unseen and purely and simply alien is not appropriated by freedom when it grasps something specific and clearly defined. Nevertheless what is unexpressed and unformulated is not necessarily absolutely unseen and unwilled. God and Christ's grace are in everything as the secret essence of all reality that is an object of choice. As a consequence, it is not very easy to seek anything without having to do with God and Jesus Christ in one way or another. Even if someone who is still far from any explicit and verbally formulated revelation accepts his human reality, his humanity, in silent patience, or rather in faith, hope and love (however he may name these), as a mystery which loses itself in the mystery of eternal love and bears life in the very midst of death, he is saying Yes to Jesus Christ even if he does not realize it. He is entrusting himself to something unfathomable, for God in fact has filled it with the unfathomable, that is, with himself, for the Word became flesh. If someone lets go and jumps, he falls into the depth which is actually there, not merely the depth he has measured. Anyone who accepts his human reality wholly and without reserve (and it remains uncertain who really does so) has accepted the Son of Man, because in him God accepted man.

We read in Scripture that those who love their neighbour have fulfilled the law. This is the ultimate truth because God himself has become that neighbour and so in every neighbour it is always he, one who is nearest and most distant, who is accepted and loved. The reality which the Christian confesses to be that of Jesus Christ is not truth and redemptive reality for him alone, it is salvation for all, provided it is not rejected in personal guilt. It 'holds true not only for Christians, but for all men of good will in whose hearts grace works in an unseen way. For, since Christ died for all men, and since the ultimate vocation of man is in fact one, and divine, we ought to believe that the Holy Spirit in a manner known only to God offers to every man the possibility of being associated with this paschal mystery' (Vatican II, *Gaudium et Spes*, art. 22).

HAVE MERCY ON US

Jesus, in the obedience that you learned in the Garden of Olives, have mercy on us.

Jesus, in the resignation that you won by your struggle in the Garden, have mercy on us.

Jesus in your readiness to suffer that was tried and proven in the Garden of Olives, have mercy on us.

Jesus, in your love for us that was not overcome in the Garden of Olives, have mercy on us.

Jesus, in your goodness that was not embittered even in the Garden of Olives, have mercy on us.

Jesus, in your courage that remained steadfast even in the Garden of Olives, have mercy on us.

Jesus, in your meekness that did not falter even in the Garden of Olives, have mercy on us.

Jesus, in the anguish and sorrow of those hours, have mercy on us.

Jesus, in your fear and trembling, have mercy on us.

Jesus, in the prayer that you offered in the Garden of Olives, have mercy on us.

Jesus, who fell prostrate on the ground, have mercy on us.

Jesus, who persevered in prayer again and again, have

mercy on us.

Jesus, whose soul was sad even unto death, have mercy on us.

Jesus, who prayed that the chalice of suffering might be taken away, have mercy on us.

Jesus, who said: 'Not my will, but thine be don' have mercy on us.

Jesus, who cried: 'Abba, Father,' have mercy on us.

Jesus, who three times said 'yes' to the will of the Father. have mercy on us.

Jesus, who was abandoned by the sleeping apostles, have mercy on us.

Jesus, who was comforted by an angel, have mercy on us;

Jesus, who suffered a bloody sweat in your agony in the Garden of Olives, have mercy on us.

Jesus, who knew and suffered in advance all future sufferings, have mercy on us.

Jesus, who knew the sins of the whole world in the Garden of Olives, have mercy on us.

Jesus, who felt disgust at the sins of all ages, have mercy on us.

Jesus who knew my sins in the Garden of Olives, have mercy on us.

Jesus, whose heart was saddened by my sins in the Garden of Olives, have mercy on us.

Jesus, who was willing to take all this upon yourself in the Garden of Olives, have mercy on us.

Jesus, whose heart was grieved by the fruitlessness of your suffering, have mercy on us.

Jesus, who felt abandoned by God during your agony in the Garden of Olives, have mercy on us.

Jesus, who was obedient to the incomprehensible will of the Father, have mercy on us.

Jesus, whose love for God never wavered though he

seemed only to be angry, have mercy on us.

Jesus, who in the Garden of Olives prayed for all who would ever suffer, have mercy on us.

Jesus, who in the Garden of Olives was the most abandoned of all the abandoned, have mercy on us.

Jesus, who in the Garden of Olives spoke for all who cry out to God from their anguish, have mercy on us.

Jesus, who in the Garden of Olives set an example for all who suffer temptation, have mercy on us.

Jesus, who in the Garden of Olives gave comfort to all who struggle painfully in the agony of death, have mercy on us.

Jesus, who in the Garden of Olives was the head of all who must suffer for the sins of the world, have mercy on us.

Jesus, who in the Garden of Olives shared as a brother in the distress and despair of the whole world, have mercy on us.

Jesus, who in the Garden of Olives understood all suffering, have mercy on us.

Jesus, who in the Garden of Olives offered a haven to all who are forsaken, have mercy on us.

Jesus, who in the Garden of Olives still loved every sinner, have mercy on us.

Jesus, who in the Garden of Olives still wanted to press to your heart the most condemned, have mercy on us.

Jesus, whose agony in the Garden of Olives redeemed our death and made it a happy homecoming, have mercy on us.

Jesus in the Garden of Olives, be merciful to us: spare us, O Jesus.

Jesus in the Garden of Olives, be merciful to us: deliver us, O Jesus.

From the sins that you wept for in the Garden of Olives, deliver us, O Jesus.

From ingratitude for your love, deliver us, O Jesus.

From indifference to your suffering, deliver us O Jesus.

From a lack of compassion for your agony and death, deliver us, O Jesus.

From resistance to the grace that you won for us in the Garden of Olives, deliver us, O Jesus.

From rejecting your acceptance of suffering and expiation in the Garden of Olives, deliver us, O Jesus.

From doubt about God's love during our own nights in the Garden of Olives, deliver us, O Jesus.

From bitterness over our own bitter agony in the Garden of Olives, deliver us, O Jesus.

From despair in our moments of abandonment, deliver us, O Jesus.

We poor sinners, we pray you, hear us.

Forgive us our sins, we pray you, hear us.

Give us an understanding of your suffering, we pray you, hear us.

Teach us your surrender to the will of the Father in the Garden of Olives, we pray you, hear us.

Give us your perseverance in prayer during the night of your agony in the Garden, we pray you, hear us.

Give us the dispositons of your heart during those hours in the Garden of Olives, we pray you, hear us.

Grant us an understanding of penance and reparation, we pray you, hear us.

Let us recognize our suffering as a share in your holy suffering, we pray you, hear us.

Fill us with your disgust for our sins, we pray you, hear us.

Give us your strength and patience in our trials and abandonment, we pray you, hear us.

Let your courage in the face of death be with us in our own death-agony, we pray you, hear us.

Send us your consoling angel at the hour of our death, we pray you, hear us.

Teach us to watch and to pray with you always in the Garden of Olives, we pray you, hear us.

Teach us to pray when we feel weak and discouraged, we pray you, hear us.

Put into our hearts and upon our lips the name 'Father', especially when God seems to be only the Lord, the stern judge, and the incomprehensible, unapproachable God, we pray you, hear us.

Lamb of God, who takes away the sins of the world, spare us, O Lord.

Lamb of God, who takes away the sins of the world, hear us, O Lord.

Lamb of God, who takes away the sins of the world, have mercy on us.

Let us pray: Jesus, who are present here, as we consider the holy dispositions of your divine and human heart, those dispositions in which you suffered the agony in the Garden of Olives in reparation, obedience, and love, and with which you dwell among us even now, we say this prayer to you: fill our hearts with sorrow for our sins; let us in union with you take up our crosses in a spirit of penance and reparation; and grant that we may gratefully return the love that you have shown us, that love which prompted you to endure your most holy sufferings in the Garden of Olives for us sinners. Amen.

RESURRECTION

What is the place of the Resurrection, as known to the disciples and men in general, in the whole understanding of existence? There should be no attempt to analyse the first

Easter experience into its elements in order to reconstitute it subsequently. Here too the whole is more than the sum of its parts. This indivisible experience includes encounter with Jesus, who knew himself to be the Son of the incomprehensible mystery which he dared to call his Father with such astonishing assuredness, even in the dereliction of death. The experience includes the encounter with his love and fidelity, with his blameless obedience in the darkness of his death and with the Easter event itself. It is possible that at the present time we cannot clearly distinguish in the Easter event between Easter (the risen Christ) and the Easter experience of the disciples. That is to say, for us the Easter experience of the disciples is never merely a purely external means of communication (like telephone wires or telescope), which disappears as it were when we have the event itself within our grasp. The Easter faith and the Easter experience (faith and its ground) were inseparable for Jesus' disciples themselves; the ground of faith (the risen Christ) was experienced powerfully and compellingly as ground of faith only in faith itself. There are other instances of matters of experience which are really accessible, but only in the experience of another; this is all the more the case, the more important and vitally central to the individual the matter is. Indubitably we are dealing here with a different situation from that of a dependable and honest witness reporting, for example, that he saw someone jump into the water. In a case of that kind the possibility of such experience is known and intelligible to us from our own experience independently of the report. Consequently, the eyewitness's report establishes a relation to the event reported which can go beyond the equally intelligible reliability and honesty of the witness and to a certain extent becomes a direct experience. As regards Easter it is different. By the nature of the case this experience is *sui generis.* For the encounter with a person from the other world, who must 'show' himself, who no longer belongs to our space and time, who on principle is not defencelessly accessible to perception on our part, is certainly not an occurrence which we can understand on the basis of our own experience. We cannot estimate its possbilities and conditions for ourselves, so as to be in a position to apply everyday criteria to decide whether we can accept it as it occurs and is experienced here and now. Reference to the empty tomb as an event of our normal world of experience accessible to everyone is of no real avail: an empty tomb cannot attest a resurrection to perfect fulfilment, because its cause can be conceived in a variety of ways. We have no experience of the same kind as the Easter experience of the first disciples, at least if we leave out of account the 'experience of the Spirit' (Ga. 3.1ff). We are therefore dependent on the testimony of the disciples in an essentially more radical sense than in the case of the acceptance of other ocular testimony. This is not to deny that that experience itself had a structure, that the disciples could therefore distinguish and express the actual ground of their experience from the process of the experience itself: 'the ground shows itself to us and is not created by our experience'. Nor is it denied that we can somehow establish this structural distance between the cause of the experience and the experience itself: by the number of witnesses, the disproportion between their mental state and the experience undergone, the vital personal effect of the experience, etc. Nevertheless all this in no way alters the fact that the Easter experience had a unique special character absolutely incommensurable with man's other experiences, and that for this reason our relation to it cannot be classed with reports of eyewitnesses in secular matters. Without the experience of the Spirit, i.e., in this case without acceptance in faith of the meaningfulness of existence (as it is, that is, as a whole), trustful reliance on the Easter testimony of the disciples will not come about even though the former can in many cases draw its real strength from the latter and in any case only fully attains its own nature through the latter. Only those who hope can see the fulfilment of hope, and at the sign of its fulfilment hope attains the purpose of its existence. This 'circle' neither needs to be, nor can be, broken. But men called to hope for the 'resurrection' of their own flesh (which they are, and do not simply possess) can by God's grace spring into that circle. How could it be otherwise here where what has to be accomplished is a total personal commitment, not in regard to this or that matter among many others of equal importance, but in regard to what gives ultimate meaning to all human reality and which is manifested in history? Such a matter must bring its own foundation with it, even though it comprises many mutually conditioning factors, and so the experienced reality of the risen Christ provides the ground of the experience and conversely the event 'manifest' itself only to faith. It should in fact never be overlooked that the perfect fulfilment, in immediacy to God, of a human existence cannot of itself be a datum which can enter into, and be happened upon within the realm of earthly experience in space and time, but at most can 'announce' itself in face of the total decision of a human life and for it (in all its dimensions). Nor do we need to imagine what someone in the genuine totality of his human existence looks like, 'with body and soul', as we say. We can calmly admit that we cannot imagine a corporeal resurrection because, unlike, for example, the raising of the dead to life, it is not and is not intended to be the restoration of a previous state but a transformation of a radical kind (of which Paul already speaks as the condition of perfect fulfilment), through which the free act of personal life must pass if it is to find its fulfilment through the overcoming of time and the maturing of time into eternity. When we say 'bodily' resurrection, we are simply saying that we are thinking of the whole man as brought to perfect fulfilment and that in accordance with our own experience of human reality we cannot divide him into an ever-valid 'spirit' and a merely provisional 'body'.

If this is considered, what ground could there be forbidding us in the name of our moral obligation to truth to trust to the Easter experience of the first disciples? Nothing compels us to believe them, if we do not wish to, and if we remain sceptical. But there is much to justify our believing them. What is required of us is something extremely bold yet quite obvious: to venture our whole existence on its being wholly directed towards God, on its having a definite meaning, on its being capable of being saved and delivered, and on precisely this having occurred in Jesus (as the exemplary and instrumental cause), so that it is possible to believe that with regard to ourselves as the first disciples did. In them there really occurred, and absolutely, to the point of death, what we should always 'like' to do, i.e., believe. And from the depth of our being we seek the objective historical facts by which such belief can come about.

Have we a better solution of the fundamental question of the meaning of our existence? Is it really more honest or simply at bottom more cowardly sceptically to shrug our shoulders in the face of this fundamental question and yet to go on acting (by living and by endeavouring to act decently) as though the whole thing had meaning all the same? There is no need to assert that anyone who considers he cannot believe in Jesus' resurrection is not able to live with an ultimately unconditional fidelity to his conscience. But we do affirm here that someone who really does this, in harmony with or in contradiction to the actual interpretations he consciously assigns to his existence, does believe—whether he is explicitly aware of this or not—in the risen Lord, who for him is nameless. For, in the fundamental decision of his personal life, even a person of this kind aims at a whole and assured existence (in body and soul) as a transformation of its present temporal character. He therefore directs his aim into history and at most does not yet know whether history has yet reached the point which even a belief of his kind acknowledges as at least the future goal of history. In that case, however, such a belief, which we too share, need not shrink from confessing (in view of Jesus and the faith of his disciples) that the event has already taken place.

ENDURING SIGN

The Church knows that it is sacrament and testimony, not for its own salvation, but for that of the world, that it serves the God of the Covenant (which is the Church) by permitting and confessing him to be greater than itself, so that the grace of which the Church is the enduring sign is victoriously offered by God even to those who have not yet found the visible Church and who nevertheless already, without realizing it, live by its Spirit, the Holy Spirit of the love and mercy of God. The Church knows that it is only what it should be if it is a community of brothers and sisters who love one another, knows that the Church too must say: If I speak in the tongues of men and angels, but have not love, I am a noisy gong or a clanging cymbal.

HUMBLED

It is certainly possible that we could fail to put a high enough value on the grace of Christ found in the Church, but it is also possible that we could fall into the opposite error of thinking that we alone are the chosen ones, we who are inside, the sons of the kingdom. Jesus says this to us: You must be the kind of men who will not hesitate to recognize the truth, to recognize goodness, honesty, virtue, loyalty, courage, wherever they appear. You must not be party men. You must see the light wherever it shines. It may be anywhere, without prejudice to the truth of the Church. We know from our faith that God's grace is not confined to the visible Church of Christ, that God's grace comes and goes through all the alleyways of the world and finds everywhere hearts in which supernatural salvation is wrought through this faith and this grace. So we Catholics should not fall into the mistake of thinking that, because we are the children of the true Church, there can be no divine grace or love except in our hearts. We must be told again and again what this Gospel tells us, that the children of the kingdom can be among those cast out, while others who did not seem to be chosen will come from the four corners of the earth and be numbered among the elect. The grace of the true Church should make us feel humbled in two ways. First because we must admit to ourselves that we are perhaps not all that we could be if this grace were fully alive and true in us. Secondly, because it brings us no certain guarantee of election. So let us follow the example of the Lord and be open and generous in recognizing whatever is good, whatever is noble and active and admirable and alive, wherever it may be, in recognizing that grace can work also outside the visible Church. Let the grace we have received make us all the more humble and so prepare us to enjoy its fruits in eternity.

FREEDOM AND LOVE

Ultimately, a living community is supported by an unknown group of Christians who have made the break-through into the true freedom of God in faith, hope and love. All Christians are or ought to be on the way to that freedom. There must, however, be some who would never dream of telling themselves and so never dare to tell others, that they have already received the 'baptism of the Spirit' of the radical freedom of love, and who nevertheless live in a community secretly liberated and redeemed by God's grace in the deepest core of their existence. It is those people who ultimately bear the weight of the community and even of its institutions in their real task. Such people can bear a burden without complaining that it belongs to someone else. They can give without thought of a reward. They can return good for evil. They can keep silent when others chatter. They can love when love means more than the natural response to being loved. They can maintain a hopeful and never-failing love of the poor and constantly humiliated Church, which in spite of everything is the assembly of their brothers and sisters in Jesus. Such people never go astray from the Church. God demands everything of a man, even when he is endlessly patient with him. He demands a man's heart in order to give him himself, the Holy Spirit of freedom, love and the invincible hope of eternal life, which ultimately needs nothing more than God alone.

We must become such people of freedom and love. We shall do so bit by bit, drawing more and more on that centre of our lives which has already been graced by baptism and confirmation. In the jealousy of his love for us, the eternal God is content with no less. The more we become such people, possessed by the liberating Spirit of

God, the more we shall build up in our communities the living Church of God and Jesus. Let us be the Church together in patience, in hope and in faith. Let us be the Church in that love which does not pass away.

BELIEVING

On Easter night believers (that is, those who think and hope they believe, but do not know it with the same certainty) and 'unbelievers' (that is, those who think they do not have such Easter faith) embrace each other as those who hope together against all hope and despite everything. The unbeliever must be glad to his believing brother who hopes he believes, even when he himself thinks he has to interpret that belief as the most prodigious moonshine (he does not thereby imagine, we trust, that his unbelief is utterly certain and reliable). And the believer must still have the courage to tell his unbelieving brother (all the time praying himself: I do have faith, help the little faith I have): the Lord is risen, he is really risen. And he may, indeed must, hope that this unbelieving brother of his is in fact a believer in the hope which is unconditionally accepted in freedom. The Christian believer may certainly not suppress the demand also to believe expressly, which is incumbent on all. But on Easter night he must be glad above all that Jesus rose among many who hope, without being able to say what has already been said by the resurrection.

PILGRIMS

It would be unbelief if we thought we could live in the social dimension by means of a ready-made ideology, whatever it might be, which would make us the absolutely sovereign planners of our future, instead of being (weary but hopeful) pilgrims constantly searching for the way to the absolute future so that then, when we have found it, we can appropriate it to ourselves in grace and undeservedly.

OFFICE

The Church must be like a family. Differences of opinion, quarrelling that sometimes is inevitable, battle even, do not destroy solidarity and love in the family, being born of and limited by the undoubted desire all members of the one family will have to serve selflessly the common good. If clergy and laity realize that they are both in the same service of God and that both must honour his demand that every man bear witness in his own place to the grace of God which is meant for all, if clergy and laity realize that at God's judgment seat they will not be asked about their position in the Church's social structure but only about their faith, hope, and love, will be judged according to whether they have been more interested in their duties in the Church than their rights, then the relationship between the hierarchy and the rest of God's people in the Church will either remain or become satisfactory. Then the laity will take it for granted that there must be order in the community of witnesses to God's grace for the world, that there must be office-bearers who 'officially' utter the word of this witness to the world inside and outside the Church, that obedience is due them within the sphere of their competence, and patient brotherly love. Clerics for their part will understand that they are nothing but servants of this word of witness, the content of which belongs as much to everyone in the Church as to them, because it is God himself who communicates himself to everyone in grace.

76

If in addition we rightly read the 'signs of the times', then still less can there be any place now for anti-clerical or anti-lay feeling. For those signs say that a Church is coming into being where the only practical significance left to ecclesiastical office will derive from the free obedience of faith and the brotherly love of all members of the Church; that a Church is coming into being where every Catholic will rejoice and thank God if by God's grace a man is prepared to shoulder the burden of ecclesiastical office, which will bring him no earthly honour or advantage.

Ecclesiastical office as such is a very ordinary matter—so ordinary that it only characterizes the pilgrim Church of this age, must be accounted part of the 'form of this world', as the Second Vatican Council explicitly declares. Therefore it will cease when this history does, having done its work. But what this office attests—communicated in the efficacious word of witness—is eternal, indeed is God himself, who has so vouchsafed himself in his glory to this finite, sinful world that the renovation of the world is already irrevocable. Office has the witness of his glory from him whom it attests, who at once exalts and humbles office. A man invested with such an office may and must say with the Apostle: 'For what we preach is not ourselves, but Christ as Lord, with ourselves as your servants for Jesus' sake . . . But we have this treasure in earthen vessels, to show that the transcendent power belongs to God and not to us.' (2 Cor 4.5, 7).

CHURCH OF ETERNITY

Not the whole life of the Christian although he is always and everywhere a member of the Church and exercises in everything a representative and sanctifying function for her, can be lived in the official and public domain of the Church as though it belonged to this and was a part of the formal accomplishment of the Church's nature in magisterium and sacraments and so on. But the existence of such a 'private' Christian life in the members of the Church does not prevent there being an intrinsic similarity and a very close connexion between their 'private' Christian life and their official, public life in the celebration of the liturgy and reception of the sacraments. If in addition we remember that even in sacramental life the personal element is not replaced or really made easy or diminished, but, in adults, should find expression in the sacraments; and that a sacrament visibly manifests in time, within the Church, before her eyes and for the world, not only the action of God and of the Church, but the interior act of the recipient's faith; it is clear that the sacraments contain implicit directions for the structure of the whole of Christian life even in its private domain. It would in fact be possible to sketch out a theology of Christian life in the concrete, on the basis of the sacraments. And since they all have an ecclesiological aspect, it would become clearer from it, that no one lives to himself; that each must bear another's burden; and that those who love their neighbour have fulfilled the law. Even in the most private sphere we are still one another's debtors. We are saved when we have forgotten ourselves on account of others. We are in blessedness when we have become those who, in the eternal kingdom of love, have found the Church of eternity, the beginning and promise of which is the Church who accomplishes her own life in the sacraments of Christ.

CHURCH AND SALVATION

If it is true to say that the Church as the continuance of Christ's presence in the world, is the fundamental sacrament of the eschatologically triumphant mercy of God, then salvation is offered and promised to the individual by his entering into positive relation to the Church. This positive relationship may possibly have very different degrees and grades of intensity, but if the individual is to attain salvation, can never entirely be lacking. God's life is offered to men plainly and once and for all in Christ, through whose incarnation the people of God exists. This has socially organized form in the Church, which is consequently the abiding and historically manifest presence of this saving grace in Christ, the fundamental sacred sign or sacrament of this grace. From this the necessity of the Chruch for salvation—at root it is the necessity of Christ himself—directly follows. Its necessity as a means is also clear, the kind of necessity which is presupposed by the question of a moral claim to men's obedience. We have also, of course, in the distinction between the aspect: people of God, and the aspect: juridical constitution of that people, within the one complete unity of the Church, an objective means of discerning degrees of intensity in membership of the Church so that in fact there can be no instance of saving grace of which one would have to say, that it had no connexion with the Church and with membership of the Church. So though the individual, in what concerns his own personal sanctification, works out his own unique, irreplaceable salvation in personal freedom, he always does so by finding his way to the Church. For the Church is the presence of saving grace in the world. To deny the ecclesiastical character of all grace and redemption would either imply that grace is not always related to the incarnation, to history and so to the Church, or else it would imply that one can attain salvation without the grace of Christ.

SPIRIT OF CHANGE

We think we seek the Holy Spirit of freedom, and seek only the genie that loads man with the chains of his own self-seeking while freeing him from others, instead of leading to the freedom of the Spirit in love for God that is purged of selfishness. Supposedly we seek the Spirit of holy joy and in fact demand the quiet enjoyment which spares us having to weep Christ's tears with him. Supposedly we seek the life-giving Spirit, and in fact we want the spirit that tells us lies about life where there is only death, so as to lure us past the life that is won by death. If we daily revise our thought in Him, if we do not misinterpret our experiences in life to mean that God's Spirit himself has grown enfeebled and has withdrawn to a distance, but learn from them that we constantly look in the wrong places and in the wrong way, that we are constantly trying to confuse Him with something else, then time and time again we shall have the heart-stirring happiness of realizing: Here he is, he is with me, the Spirit of faith in obscurity, the Spirit of victory through weakness, the Spirit of freedom in obedience, the Spirit of joy in tears, the Spirit of eternal life in the midst of death. Then, for all the earthly improbability and the stillness with which the Spirit works in us and in the Church, the holy certainty will fill us: Here he is, he is with me, he prays with me with 'sighs too deep for words', he consoles and strengthens, he sancti-fies and sustains, he gives the confidence of eternity. But we must renew our thinking daily, daily we must allow ourselves to be changed by the Spirit of change.

COMMUNITY OF THE PEOPLE OF GOD

The Church is not a mythical entity to be hypostasized or personified in a false way. By the will of Christ her founder she is the organized community of the people of God, established through the incarnation in the unity of the one human race. Even if such a society is represented by individual human beings, it still remains a community. Such a collectivity may in a true sense continue in being even when all its members are asleep and the common business or activity for the moment has completely ceased. But in order to exist, nevertheless, a community has to fulfil its nature, must actually function. The enduring existence of such a society can to be sure find concrete expression in the most diverse ways, and manifest itself with greater or less intensity in visible historical form. And a community of spiritual persons depends much more than a real individual person on such *actus secundi* (operations flowing from a nature and expressing it), because it is only an association. One can confidently say that once a society once and for all its own actualization and functioning, it would by that very fact cease to exist altogether. That holds true of the Church too. The Church exists in the full sense, in the highest degree of actual fulfilment of her nature, by teaching, bearing witness to Christ's truth, bearing the cross of Christ through the ages, loving God in her members, rendering present in rite in the sacrifice of the mass the saving grace that is hers.

ORGANIZATION

The Church is not merely a religious institution, established to meet religious needs. It goes without saying that it was not created by men for that purpose. But neither was it simply founded from above by Christ as a spiritual welfare establishment. The institutional, hierarchical build of the Church with its legal and official organization, which, of course, exists and is essential to the Church and shares in the indispensability of the Church for salvation, is the juridical constitution of something that must be already there for it to be given such a constitution. The reality that has to be so organized and constituted, with a basis in a hierarchical and juridical order that is its expression, is not the amorphous mass of individual human beings in need of redemption, but the 'people of God'. It is because this is what it is, not what it has yet to become, that it receives in the Church as a juridical organization its institutional structure according to Christ's will at its foundation.

PRINCIPLES AND PRESCRIPTIONS

The Church is not simply of herself in possession of all the prescriptions that are practically and morally important for the individual and for states and nations. She does not impose on anyone, for example, his trade or profession and is indubitably incompetent in principle to do so, even though such a prescription is of the greatest importance for the individual and his salvation and even for herself, when there is a shortage of priests, for instance. She also expressly disclaims any direct competence in temporal matters, in the secular decisions of peoples and states, in constitutional economic cultural questions and so on. If she does ascribe to herself in these things an 'indirect power' (however this may be more exactly defined), in view of the moral importance of such decisions, and if by the moral law which she proclaims she puts limits to what is morally permissible in such decisions, that clearly presupposes once again that her principles and her power to forbid some concrete decisions as immoral, leave open in principle a domain within which several decisions are possible from the abstract ethical point of view. And it would not be possible for the Church herself to say which of these is the one to choose, the right one, the historically successful one. Yet the choice between these several alternatives cannot be dismissed as indifferent and unimportant, for on just this choice, which the Church declares beyond her own competence, everything may historically depend, the rise or fall of a nation or a civilization. It by no means follows from the fact that no contradiction to the general precepts of morality and therefore to their administration by the Church can be detected, that everything will certainly be avoided that might turn out historically disastrous. Otherwise, for example, the morally blameless and ecclesiastically dutiful statesman would necessarily be right in fact and historically successful in his decisions.

It follows that in the life of the individual and of nations, the Church recognizes a domain of decisions, concrete individual accomplishments and consequently of prescriptions, for which as such she has no competence. This domain lies outside the scope of general principles and the Church's pastoral power. She does not and cannot relieve the individual or nations of the task of discovering such prescriptions nor of the burden of deciding. Salutary and beneficial as the general principles are which she preaches, she leaves individuals and nations, in regard to these particular prescriptions, to their own devices; they themselves must engage in the struggle to discover, choose and carry them out. Now of these, one can be the correct one, appropriate to the age and moment and the historical individuality of the agent, another can be quite the wrong one, though both may conform to general moral principles. It may not be possible to say that this only seems to be so, that in fact this apparent conformity stems not from the facts but from the agent's limited knowledge, acting as seemed good to him but objectively and in relation to general moral principles acting incorrectly.

The Church does not administer all reality. Everything indeed belongs to the kingdom of God, but not to the Church that prepares the way for the kingdom. The Church cannot say whether in France after 1871 the Bonapartists or the Monarchists or the Republicans were 'right' in their prescriptions. She could enunciate neither the one nor the other of those prescriptions; she could only say that *suppositis supponendis* each of them was compatible with the general moral principles of which she is the guardian. But this would not settle whether one was historically right and the other not, nor would it settle whether all three would entail more or less the same consequence for the Church herself, the kingdom of God and the salvation of souls.

THE SPIRIT OF PRIESTHOOD

Lord Jesus Christ, Son of the living God, eternal Word of the Father, high priest of all men.

We thank you for being pleased to prepare us for your priesthood.

We confess that *you* have chosen us, not we you, that without your grace we should be unworthy and feeble and unfit to follow such a vocation. But you have prepared us. We are to be your witnesses. We thank you, angel of great counsel. We are to proclaim your truth. We praise you, O Word of eternal truth. We are to renew your sacrifice. We praise you, priest and victim forever. We are to dispense your grace. We bless you, incarnate clemency of the Father, and give you heartfelt thanks for calling us into your sanctuary, to your altar, and to your own priestly mission. We give you thanks. You spoke for us too when you came into the world. I too have come to do your will, a body you have prepared for me. You besought God for us too when you prayed all night long for your Apostles before choosing them. With us too you were patient and clement when you bore with your uncomprehending disciples. You rejoiced over our work too when you blessed the Father at the disciples' homecoming. For us too you anxiously prayed that our faith should not waver and we should be strengthened in Peter, when Satan lusts to sift us like the wheat. We too were in your mind when you gave the Apostles the law of their life in the Sermon on the Mount and the epitome of their prayer in the Our Father.

You included us when you said to your Apostles: Let not your hearts be troubled; why are you afraid, O men of little faith? I appointed you that you should go and bear fruit, a servant is not greater than his master, whoever does not renounce all that he has cannot be my disciple. In your Apostles you have called us your friends, your little children, your brothers, as dear to you as brother and sister and mother. Your word was meant to reach our hearts too when you spoke these words to your Apostles and a thousand more, which your Gospel hands on to us as your bequest to your priests and which we should read on our knees and in tears. You had us too in mind when you uttered words before which all the principalities and powers of history quake and fall prostrate: Go and make disciples of all nations, baptizing them: do this in remembrance of me; if you forgive the sins of any, they are forgiven; whatever you loose on earth shall be loosed in heaven. O Jesus, priest and king forever, it is your will that we be and remain your priests. Be blessed forever.

Lord, we would always be beginning anew to become what you have already called us to be. We shall go back joyful and courageous to the daily life where we are to mature still more into apostles and priests of your holdy Church. Give us your Holy Spirit, therefore, and the spirit of your priesthood for this new pilgrimage of ours, the spirit of reverence towards God, the spirit of contrition, the spirit of holiness and chaste fear of dishonouring the holy God by sin, the spirit of faith and love of prayer, the spirit of purity and manly discipline, the spirit of knowledge and wisdom, the spirit of brotherly love and concord beyond all envy and strife, the spirit of joy and confidence, the spirit of magnanimity and generosity, the spirit of obedience, patience, and love of your holy cross. On this road let us have God your Father before our eyes, let us walk in his holy presence, work honestly to teach our hearts, stick together among ourselves fraternally, share one another's burden and thus fulfil your law.

Let us grow daily more and more like you through true, constant, selfless spiritual effort and struggle, O you the eternal wisdom of God!

Grant us, above all, the grace of prayer and mke us love you, O Jesus. What are we without you? Lost. We can only have you if we make you, by love and prayer, again and again and more and more the focus of our heart. If you want us to be your priests, then grant us, O Lord, that gift without which we cannot truly be your priests. Grant us the grace of prayer, of collection, of inwardness, stop us when we want to run away from you in our distraction and absent-mindedness; bring us crazy people back to you, if need be by the prick of pain, the bitterness of heart and of distress. Give us just one gift: the grace to pray truly and to become daily more. When we pray, we are and remain in fellowship with you, then we shall increasingly become what we are and ought to be according to your will: your disciples, your apostles, your priests, the witnesses of your truth and the dispensers of your mysteries.

We have given ourselves and you the pledge to become your priests: just priests and nothing besides, priests in undivided service. You look at us, your eyes pierce through our conscience, your love touches our heart. And you say: You are my friends if you do what I command you (Jn 15. 14). But we dare to look up to you humbly and trustingly and to say: by your grace we will be what you have commanded us to be. Amen.

COPING

We are not the masters of our history. We must accept the age and the hour as they are given to us. Our life is not always faced with the same demand, the same testing. So we Christians today, who proclaim the faith of the Church of Jesus Christ, are asked—and ask ourselves—in quite new, searching ways whether and how we are still believers. In former times faith was simply the most obvious presupposition of our office. Now that presupposition, that faith we shared with everyone almost as a matter of course, is suddenly becoming something like the central feature of office, even the primal and decisive act of office. It is alarming to be asked for so exhaustive an explanation. And so the first point to be made is that we must accept this situation coolly and without embarrassment. We must come to realize that for faith to be threatened and assaulted, to have to be conceived and accomplished anew every day, is not an unnatural condition fortuitously thrust upon it by outward calamities, but part of the quintessence of faith. Outward circumstances with which we and our faith have to cope only remind us once more what faith is of itself.

PERFECT

The word 'perfect' in Greek, as in English, implies that an end has been reached. The perfect law only exists complete and glorious when we ourselves have reached our end, have ceased to endure this finitude and are perfected in the un-veiled freedom of God's children. Then we are wholly liberated. But James says that we are to live even now in the perfect law of liberty. And so that law must be given to us in this world, to us poor, indigent, suffering, limited, finite souls in this poor world. Yes, it is already given to us, for God's Spirit, the Spirit of infinite freedom, is already given to us—in faith, of course; in hope; and in that love which will never end. If then we feel unfree, imprisoned, distressed, and heavy laden, that is an admonition to descend deeper into our hearts, to where God already dwells in his Holy Spirit of boundless freedom. It is an admonition to pray: I believe in the perfect law of liberty, I believe in eternal life, I believe in God the liberator, in the truth of God which sets men free, in the love of God which is free. Then, doing the works of faith, we shall not feel distressed to be still in chains, because in our heart of hearts we are already liberated, and so we know that everything which still keeps us unfree is transitory, and that the perfect law of freedom endures for all eternity.

SCRIPTURE

Dogmatic theology cannot avoid engaging in biblical theology. For dogmatic theology is a systematic, deliberate attention to God's revelation in Jesus Christ. It is not merely a theology of conclusions drawn from the principles of faith assumed as premises, as medieval theology theoretically conceived itself to be through its real practice was quite different. Consequently dogmatic theology must listen most attentively to revelation where the most direct and ultimate source of Christian revelation is to be found, namely in Scripture. Of course dogmatic theology always reads Scripture under the guidance of the magisterium, because it reads Scripture in the Church, and therefore instructed by the Church's present proclamation of the faith.

It follows that theology always reads Scripture with a knowledge which is not simply to be found in that precise form in Scripture. The theologian has always to study his theology on the basis of the Church's present awareness of its faith. And there has been a genuine development of dogma. Nevertheless theology has not simply the task of expounding the present teaching of the faith by the Church's magisterium and of showing it to be justified from Scripture by finding *dicta probantia* for it there. Its own function as dogmatic theology in regard to Scripture goes beyond this process, which is unfortunately too often almost the only one. In the first place, the existing Church itself is always reading Scripture, reading it to the faithful and ordering it to be read. It is, therefore, not the case that *only* what is taught in the Church by councils, encyclicals, catechisms, etc. belongs to the actual teaching of the Church's magisterium. Scripture itself is also what is actually officially proclaimed at all times in the Church.

Theological concern with God's revelation in the actual

teaching of the Church's magisterium, and in the mind of the Church of one's own time, inevitably leads back to Scripture. That is so even where that teaching is not the actual reading of Scripture in the Church of the present. The full understanding of present doctrine demands a perpetual return to the source from which, on its own admission, this doctrine is derived.

PILGRIMS

Do we not all have to admit that we are pilgrims on a journey, men who have no fixed abodes, even though we must never forget our native country? How time flies, how the days dwindle down, how we are eternally in change, how we move from place to place. Somewhere, and at some time or other, we come into existence, and already we have set out on the journey that goes on and on, and never again returns to the same place. And the journey's path moves through childhood, through youthful strength and through the maturity of age, through a few festal days and many routine weekdays. It moves through heights and through misery, through purity and through sin, through love and through disillusion. On and on it goes, irresistibly on from the morning of life to the evening of death. So irresistibly, so inexorably does it move on that we often fail to notice that we fancy ourselves to be standing still, because we are always on the move and because everything else also seems to be going along with us, everything else that we have somehow managed to include in the course of our life.

GROWING OLD

Old age is a grace (= both mission and risk) not given to everyone, just as, in the Christian understanding, there are other possibilities and situations reckoned as graces which are granted to some and withheld from others. That must be seen and accepted as part of 'God's will'. In this connexion we should not take facile comfort in the ultimately erroneous thought that old age, like many other life situations, is a merely external situation which does not terminate in the definitive sequel of life but is merely like a costume in which a person plays a role in the theatre of life which remains extraneous to himself, which he simply drops at death, which does not—even transformed—end in the personal definitiveness we call eternal life. Such an opinion (only superficially pious) does not take man's history really seriously: 'eternity' is the (transformed) definitiveness of history itself. Whether a person dies young or old, he takes this temporal destiny of his into his definitiveness as an inner moment of it.

Therefore growing old is a really serious matter. It is a grace, a mission and the risk of radical failure. It is a part of human and Christian life which (like every other part of life) has its insubstituable and irreplaceable importance. That is particularly true since old age must be understood not simply as life's running out but as life's 'coming to definitiveness', even when that happens under the paralyzing influence of slow, biological death. *Mutatis mutandis,* the same thing may be said of old age as is said of death in its Christian understanding. We undergo death not in medical cessation but in the length and breadth of life, with all its different phases.

DYING

Knowledge, even if mostly an implicit knowledge, of the inevitability of death, though not of its when and where, intrinsically determines the whole of life. In this knowledge death is always already present in human life and only by this does life assume its full gravity, through the necessity of its activities, the uniqueness of its opportunities and the irrevocability of its decisions. Just as personal failure before the absolute claim experienced in conscience is the most poignant, so death is the most tangible expression of man's finitude. But precisely in the explicitly conscious presentiment of death in natural mortal anguish it is apparent that life itself points limitlessly beyond death. For in mortal anguish death does not appear (as in the mere fear of death) only as a possibly painful single event at the end of life, but rather as an event of such a kind that in fact of it man is freed from his attachment to all that is individual and he is confronted with the truth, namely, that in death the fundamental decision which a man has made in regard to God, the world and himself, and which dominates his whole life, receives its definitive character. Man hopes that at the same time it means fulfilment, yet he remains uncertain whether this is achieved. The will of man maturing from within to the totality and finality of his attitude of life is always alienated by the dispersion of bodily existence and is robbed of its power of disposing of all in a coherent whole. He therefore cannot bring to open, unambiguous certainty the totality of a definitively composed personal life which he strives for. Consequently the act of human life remains essentially impenetrable in face of death, threatened from without, and in death finally comes to its sharpest contradiction, the simultaneity of highest will and extreme weakness, a lot which is actively achieved and passively suffered, plentiude and emptiness.

This fundamentally obscure and ambiguous situation of death is the consequence of original sin which affects all men and becomes in them a natural expression of the fall of man in Adam from his grace-given immortality, the clear fulfilment of an earthly existence transfigured by communion with God. According to whether a man wills autonomously to understand and master this death, due to original sin and beyond his clear power of control, which he accomplishes as a personal action throughout life, or whether he holds himself open in death with unconditional readiness in faith for the incomprehensible God, his death will become either a personal repetition and confirmation of the sinful emancipation of the first humsn being and so the culmination of sin, definitive mortal sin, or it will be the personal reptition and appropriation of Christ's obedient death by which Christ inserted his divine life into the world itself. In this way it becomes the culmination of man's salutary activity. Conformation to the death of Christ, anticipated throughout life in faith and sacraments, is now personally accomplished and becomes a final blessed 'dying in the Lord', in which the experience of the end becomes the dawn of perfect fulfilment.

ROSES CAN BE BLACK

Teresa of Lisieux died in the mortal temptation of empty absolute unbelief, and still believed; believed as she choked with consumption; to her all the pious fuss of her fellow sisters must have been unutterably empty and painful. Here is someone who died *accepting* as a destructive reality what had been devoutly talked over; what she must have strongly suspected of being a dream world into which a young thing escaped because it was frightened of reality and truth, something that looked as if it belonged to the plush furniture with which the parents of the 'Little Flower' crammed their living-room.

You could object that a great many people die like that. Whether in a modern aseptic clinic, abandoned by loved ones who slip away helplessly; or under napalm bombs; or—oh, I do not know, people are dying everywhere, and should I not believe, hoping desperately against hope, that there, if you scrape away from this multifarious death everything that is bourgeois, miserable and pompous, there is still a death in which a person lets himself go, with the courage of faith, hope and love, into the incomprehensible (whom we all God) so that what is really happening is valuable enough to remain for ever? Does it always happen? I don't know. I hope so. I hope it does, although only the misery and the disillusionment of human life effectively appear in death.

What is there about Teresa's death which really interests me, which is special, once we discount the pious ferment surrounding it (to which I have no objection, but which I cannot take so seriously), and for which her environment and even her own petty-bourgeois Christian education were responsible? To this question I give an answer which I imagine will shock most people who are not ecclesially domesticated: because I really trust that *this* death was successful (in the sense just suggested), what I otherwise do not know with the same certainty I trust is true *because* the Church has understood and guaranteed *this* successful death.

Devout *and* undevout turmoil round a death are very ambiguous and of questionable importance. Someone can die a dignified death declaring he is an atheist and with polite thanks reject the pastor's endeavours. Or he can die with the entire panoply of Christian church ceremonial, and want this, and be happy and consoled by it. (Let the Pecksmiffs of orthodoxy note that I do *not* equate these two situations,)

We know from the old catechism what *should* result in the case of death, yet in *neither* of these cases can we know what *did* result; not even, in an exact and quite serious sense, when we can say so much that is genuinely edifying about a death (even apart from pious glosses), as is the case with St Teresa. That is because we do not know of anyone *how* he let himself go into the incomprehensible; whether with a willing (beatifying) surrender or with a final protest —which, because of the dignity of freedom, I must also believe is possible. But now the Church tells me that here a death has succeeded as an act of faith. When I say 'Church', I do not mean merely, or even primarily, the official declaration of Rome at the canonization: ultimately, that is no more than an echo of the Church's conviction: of this Church of praying, calling, trusting, and praising Christians.

It does not greatly worry me that the Church's conviction (in that sense) has appeared in such shoddy and infantile forms. That is always the case when a crowd has to do and does something in common. But I trust to those countless Christians for a genuine insight into where that which is genuine and eternal happens. And I accept it confidently as the discernment of spirits (of deaths) which takes place in the Holy Spirit. Once such a death is recognized for what it really and almost impalpably *was*, the statues of little saints with their roses in the niches of many churches can gather dust once again. It is nonetheless true that a person's death succeeds in darkness as the ascent of light, conquering all unbelief and despair.

That is the sort of message I understand. It has the weight of eternity which comes to every human life. I can also accept it in regard to other people who have died and who show that one can really die with Jesus, accepting unutterable loneliness as God's saving hand. I can also say it of Teresa of Lisieux, who died three years before Nietzsche (and he thought that God—and true man with him—was dead and could not rise again).

The answer has run ahead of the question. The answer can make the question intelligible to Christians yet be a real answer. Roses can be black. They can fall further into the night of death; black roses of hope falling inaudibly, almost indistinguishably; falling into your night, and mine.

THE LORD'S DEATH

If the dead live, if the departed are not those whose life has melted into the void but rather those whose history has found its finality in God, we have the right and the sacred duty again and again to confess the validity of their lives of all those who have preceded us in the sign of faith. In this we also confess her whose soul the sword of pain pierced, who again according to Luke was blessed because she believed. When we confess the law of her life, the law of her faith, we are calling on her, and we are paying her homage as the model of all believers.

We celebrate the memory of the Lord's death. We thereby confess that we do not wish to accept the sword of our existence, wherever and in whatever form it comes, as if we had no hope. We celebrate the Lord's death in worship and festival so that we can celebrate it in the blessed bitterness of life, in us, around us and also in our knowing, which cannot be perfected this side of death. Let us proclaim the Lord's death until he comes.

LIFE WITH THE DEAD

Since your love is infinite, it can abide only in your infinity; and since you will to manifest your infinite love to me, you have hidden it in my finiteness, where you issue your call to me. My faith in you is nothing but the dark path in the night between the abandoned hut of my poor, dim earthly life and the brilliance of your eternity. And your silence in this time of my pilgrimage is nothing but the earthly manifestation of the eternal word of your love.

That is how my dead imitate your silence: they remain hidden from me because they have entered into your life. The words of their love no longer reach my ears, because they are conjoined with the jubilant song of your endless love. My dead live the unhampered and limitless life that you live; they love with your love; and thus their life and their love no longer fit into the frail and narrow frame of my present existence. I live a dying life—*prolixitas mortis* is the Church's name for this life—so how can I expect to experience their eternal life, which knows no death?

And that is also the way they live for me. Their silence is their loudest call to me, because it is the echo of your silence. Their voice speaks in unison with yours, trying to make itself heard above the noisy tumult of our incessant activity, competing with the anxious protestations of mutual love with which we poor humans try to reassure each other. Against all this, their voice and yours strive to enwrap us and all our words in your eternal silence.

Thus your word summons us to enter into your life. Thus you command us to abandon ourselves by the daring act of love which is faith, so that we may find our eternal home in your life. And thus I am called and commanded by the silence of my dead, who live your life and therefore speak your word of the God of life, so far removed from my dying. They are silent because they live, just as we chatter so loudly to try to make ourselves forget that we are dying. Their silence is really their call to me, the assurance of their immortal love for me.

O silent God, God of the silent dead, living God of the living, who call to me through silence, O God of those who are silently summoning me to enter into your life, never let me forget my dead, my living. May my love and faithfulness to them be a pledge of my belief in you, the God of eternal life.

Let me not be deaf to the call of their silence, which is the surest and sincerest word of their love. May this word of theirs continue to accompany me, even after they have taken leave of me to enter into you, for thus their love comes all the closer to me. O my soul, never forget your dead, for they live. And the life they live, now unveiled in eternal light, is your own life, which will one day be revealed also in you.

O God of the living, may your living not forget me, as I still walk in the valley of death. You have granted them everything, even yourself; grant them this too, that their silence may become the most eloquent word of their love for me. May it lead me home to the kingdom they now possess, to the life and light they now enjoy.

My waning life is becoming more and more a life with the dead. I live more and more with those who have gone before me into the dark night where no man can work. By your life giving grace, O Lord, let is become ever more a life in your light, shining now dimly in this earthly night. Let me live with the living who have preceded me in the sign of faith, who have gone before me into the bright day of eternal life, when no man need work, because you yourself are this day, the fulness of all reality, the God of the living.

When I pray: 'Grant them eternal rest, O Lord, and let

thy perpetual light shine upon them,' let my words be only the echo of the prayer of love that they themselves are speaking for me in the silence of eternity: 'O Lord, grant unto him, who we love in your love now as never before, grant unto him after his life's struggle your eternal rest, and let your perpetual light shine also upon him, as it does upon us.'

O my soul, never forget the dead. O God of all the living, do not forget me, the dead one, but come one day to be my life, as you are theirs.

BEGINNING OF DEATH

In Jesus, surrender to everlasting mystery is there as a human act, which is itself grace—like everything that is freedom and decision. In Jesus God, as the unutterable mystery (which he remains), has expressed himself wholly and irrevocably as the word. In Jesus the word is there, as something addressed to us all, as the God of closeness, of unutterable intimacy and forgiveness. In Jesus there is question. In Jesus there is answer. Unmixed and yet inseparable, question and answer have become one. The One is there in whom God and man are one, without any reciprocal cancellation. His self-surrender to mystery is borne by mystery itself. It is not only an action of theory and emotion, but the act of life as a whole in all its dimensions. Therefore it finds its absolute culmination in his death, in which he voluntarily allows himself to fall as it were into the final coming of the mystery before which man is trustingly silent. For Jesus as for us, therefore, Christmas is the beginning of death.

ACCEPTANCE OF PASSION

Lent is the religious explicitness of that period of 'fast' and 'passion' which extends over our whole lives. Today's welfare and consumer state has accommodated itself to a permanent lie: the impression is universally given that serene happiness is everywhere the rule, or if that is not strictly true in every case, it soon will be with good will and the irresistible progress of mankind. Evidently no one would wish to quarrel with the ideals of more health, freedom and so on by which modern man sets such store. The fact is that many things remain: pain, old age, sickness, disappointment in marriage, in the children, in one's job, and at the end of it all death, which no one escapes and which is already a controlling, permeating factor of life. The question can consequently be only *how* one is to cope with this reality of suffering and death.

Cynicism and stoicism do not go very far. In faith, hope and love a Christian understands this aspect of his life as a sharing in the Lord's passion. The acceptance in belief and hope of one's own passion is exercised by what in Christian asceticism is called 'voluntary renunciation'. In Lent, however, that which one must necessarily suffer in life in sober realism and can live in hope as a *Christian* passion becomes publicly known, in ecclesial, liturgical and sacramental explicitness, as a freely-loving participation in the passion of Christ.

I COMMEND MY SPIRIT

O Jesus utterly forsaken, tormented by suffering, you have come to the end. To that end where everything is taken away, even one's soul and his freedom to say 'yes' or 'not', and hence where man is taken from himself. For that is what death is. Who or what does the taking? Nothing? Blind fate? Merciless nature? No, it is the Father! God, who is wisdom and love! And so you let yourself be taken from yourself. You give yourself over with confidence into those gentle, invisible hands. We who are weak in faith and fearful for our own selves experience those hands as the sudden, grasping, merciless, stifling grip of blind fate and of death. But you know that they are the hands of the Father. And your eyes, now grown dark in death, can still see the Father. They look up into the large, peaceful eyes of his love, and from your lips come the last words of your life: 'Father, into your hands I commend my spirit.'

You give everything to him who gave everything to you. You put everything into the hands of your Father without guarantee and without reservations. That is doing a great deal, and it is a hard and bitter thing to do. All alone you had to bear the burden of your life: all men, their meanness, your mission, your cross, failure and death. But now the time for enduring is past. Now you can put everything and yourself into the hands of the Father. Everything. Those hands are so gentle and so sure. They are like the hands of a Mother. They embrace your soul as one would like a little bird carefully and lovingly into his hands. Now nothing is difficult any more, everything is easy, everything is light and grace. And everything is safe and secure in the heart of God, where one can cry all his anguish out, and the Father will kiss away the tears from the cheeks of his child.

O Jesus, will you one day put my poor soul and my poor life also into the hands of the Father? Put everything there, the burden of my life, and the burden of my sins, not on the scales of justice, but into the hands of the Father. Where should I flee, where should I seek refuge, if not at your side? For you are my brother in bitter moments, and you suffered for my sins. See, I come to you today. I

101

kneel beneath your cross. I kiss the feet which follow me down the wandering path of my life constantly and silently, leaving bloody footprints behind.

I embrace your cross, Lord of eternal love heart of all hearts, heart that was pierced, heart that is patient and unspeakably kind. Have mercy on me. Receive me into your love. And when I come to the end of my pilgrimage, when the day begins to decline and the shadows of death surround me, speak your last word at the end of my life also: 'Father, into your hands I commend his spirit.' O good Jesus. Amen.

BLISS WITHOUT END

Oh, grow in me, enlighten me, shine forth ever stronger in me, eternal light, sweet light of my soul. Sound out in me ever more clearly, O word of the Father, word of love, Jesus. You've said that you have revealed to us all you have heard from the Father. And your word is true, for what you have heard from the Father is you yourself, O word of the Father. You are the word which knows itself and the Father. And you are mine, O word beyond all human words, O light before whom all earthly light is only night's blackness.

May you alone enlighten me, you alone speak to me. May all that I know apart from you be nothing more than a chance travelling companion on the journey toward you. May it help to mature me, so that I may ever better understand you in the suffering that it brings me, as your holy writer has predicted. When it has accomplished this, then it can quietly disappear into oblivion.

Then you will be the final word, the only one that remains, the one we shall never forget. Then at last, everything will be quiet in death; then I shall have finished with all my learning and suffering. Then will begin the great silence, in which no other sound will be heard but you, O word resounding from eternity to eternity.

Then all human words will have grown dumb. Being and knowing, understanding and experience will have become one and the same. 'I shall know even as I am known'; I shall understand what you have been saying to me all along, namely, you yourself. No more human words, no more concepts, no more pictures will stand between us. You yourself will be the one exultant word of love and life filling out every corner of my soul.

Be now my consolation, O Lord, now when all knowledge, even your revelation expressed in human language, fails to still the yearning of my heart. Give me strength, O God, now when my soul easily tires of all the human words we devise about you, words which still fail to give us the possession of you. Even though the few flashes of light I receive in quiet moments quickly fade out again into the dark-grey sky of my daily life—even though knowledge comes to me now only to sink back again into oblivion, still your word lives in me, of which it is written: 'The word of the Lord abides forever'.

You yourself are my knowledge, the knowledge that is light and life. You yourself are my knowledge, experience, and love. You are the God of the one and only knowledge that is eternal, the knowledge that is bliss without end.

SILENT GOD

God is silent just like the dead. For us to celebrate his feasts in our hearts, this silent God must certainly be with us, even though he seems so distant and so silent. We certainly must love him, as we love our dead, the distant and silent dead, who have entered into the night. Does he not give to our love an intelligible answer when we call him to the feast of the heart, and ask him for a sign that his love exists for us and is present to us? And that is why we cannot lament the silence of the dead, for their silence is only an echo of his silence.

But if we keep silent and meek, if we listen to this silence of God's, then we begin to grasp with a comprehension that exceeds our own power to evoke or even to understand why both God and the dead are so silent. Then it dawns on us that they are near us precisely in our feast of the holy souls.

God's silence is the boundless sphere where alone our love can produce its act of faith in his love. If in our earthly life his love had become so manifest to us that we would know beyond a shadow of a doubt what we really are, namely God's own beloved, then how could we prove to him the daring courage and fidelity of our love? How could such a fidelity exist at all? How could our love, in the ecstasy of faith, reach out beyond this world into his world and into his heart? He has veiled his love in the stillness of his silence so that our love might reveal itself in faith. He has apparently forsaken us so that we can find him.

For if his presence in our midst were obvious, in our search for him we would find only ourselves. We must, however, go out from ourselves, if we are to find him where he is really himself. Because his love is infinite, it can dwell openly and radiantly only in his own infinity; and because he wants to show us his infinite love, he has hidden it from us in our finiteness, whence he calls out to us. Our faith in him is nothing but the dark road in the night between the deserted house of our life with its puny, dimly lit rooms, and the blinding light of his eternal life. His silence in this world is nothing but the earthly appearance of the eternal word of his love.

Our dead imitate this silence. Thus, through silence, they speak to us clearly. They are nearer to us than through all the audible words of love and closeness. Because they have entered into God's life, they remain hidden from us. Their words of love do not reach our ears because they have blended into one with the joyous word of his boundless love. They live with the boundlessness of God's life and with his love, and that is why their love and their life no longer enter the narrow room of our present life. We live a dying life.

BEATIFIC VISION

In theological language 'beatific vision' usually means perfect salvation in its entirety, though verbally it particularly stresses the intellectual component in the single whole which constitutes salvation. This is the full and definitive experience of the direct self-communication of God himself to the individual human being when by free grace God's will has become absolute and attained its full realization. Since this absolute will (efficacious grace of perfect salvation in predestination) attains the individual precisely as a member of redeemed humanity in Christ and because of Christ, the term also implies in the concrete, if not formally, the unity of the redeemed and perfected in the perfect Kingdom of God, 'heaven', as the communion of the blessed with the glorified Lord and his humanity, and with one another—the perfect accomplishment of the 'communion of saints'. As the definitive, irrevocable completion of God's action on man and on human freedom (which freely wills what is final), the beatific vision is 'eternal life'. The difference of 'time' (to the extent that it can and has

105

to be conceived) between the perfect fulfilment of the one human being in his spiritual and personal dimension and his perfect accomplishment in his corporeal dimension, is ultimately of little account. Scripture in fact always refers to the total fulfilment of man and simply envisages it from different aspects.

PEACE

As if by a miracle, which must be renewed every day, you will perceive that you are with God. You will suddenly experience that your God-distance is in truth only the disappearance of the world before the dawning of God in your soul, and that the darkness is nothing but God's brightness, that throws no shadow, and your *lack of outlets* is only the immeasurability of God, to whom no road is needed, because he is already there. You shall see that you should not try to run away from your empty heart, because he is already there, and so there can be no reason for you to flee from this blessed despair into consolation that would be no consolation, into a consolation that does not exist. He is there. Do not seek to hold him fast. He does not run away. Do not seek to make sure of yourself and to touch him with the hands of your greedy heart. You would only be clutching at a straw, not because he is distant and unreal, but because he is the Infinite who cannot be touched. He is there, right in the midst of your choked-up heart, he alone. But he is all, and so it appears as if he were nothing.

If we do this, then peace comes all by itself. Peace is the most genuine activity: the silence that is filled with God's word, the trust that is no longer afraid, the sureness that no longer needs to be assured, and the strength that is powerful in weakness—it is, then, the life that rises through death. There is nothing more in us then but God; God and the almost imperceptible and yet all-filling faith that he is there, and that we are.

But one thing more must still be said: this God-distance would not be the rising of God in mortal, choked-up hearts if the Son of Man, who is the Son of the Father, had not suffered and done just this with us and for us and on our behalf in his own heart. But he has suffered and done all this. It happened in the garden, from whose fruit men wanted to press out the oil of joy, the garden that was in truth the garden of the lost paradise. He lay on his face; death crept into his living heart, into the heart of the world. Heaven was locked up and the world was like a monstrous grave; and he alone in that grave, choked up by the guilt and helplessness of the world. As refreshment, the angel who looked like death passed him the cup of bitterness, that he might sink into agony. The earth wickedly and greedily gulped down the drops of blood of his mortal terror. God blanketed everything as with a night that no longer promised day. One can no longer separate him from death. In this vast death-silence—men slept, dulled by grief— in this death-silence the small voice of the Son floated somewhere, the only sign from God that was still left. Each moment it seemed to be stifled. But a great miracle took place: the voice remained. The Son spoke to the awful God with this tiny voice that was like a dead man's; 'Father'—he spoke to his own abandonment—'Thy will be done'. And in ineffable courage he commended his abandoned soul into the hands of this Father.

Ever since that moment, our poor soul, too, is laid in the hands of this God, this Father, whose former decree of death has now become love. Ever since that time, our despair is redeemed, the emptiness of our heart has become fulfilment, and God-distance has become our homeland.

107

OUR BALANCE

How is our balance doing now, at the end? There is the most reliable entry, the only one that puts the balance in order, the entry that makes us forget to ask about the result of the balance: carry on with the hard, customary, routine duties of the Christian life of good works. Carry on! Today and tomorrow. As long as it pleases God to let you carry on. Be on the lookout a little lest you allow those rare opportunities for greater good works slip by. And as long as our good works always give us a little pain and are bitter to the heart, as long as we do the next good work, in order to forget that the first was good, then we also know that this work is not yet degenerating into external routine, and that we have not grown pharisaically hard in the doing of good, in spite of our years.

Thus the balance becomes a dropping of the balance—I forget what lies behind me. The balance becomes a running after the prize of eternal life in the bitter-sweet difficulties of the Christian daily life.

When we run the course in this way, then we are allowed everything. In this course, we may even be permitted to draw up a balance, thankfully or contritely. When we run the course in this way, then some day even that awareness of having been chosen out for heaven, an awareness that steals softly and furtively, like a shadow, only through the heart's most secret chamber, may come over us. Delightful grace: already the tree of life is bending lower and lower, already it is beginning to sink down into God's land. Already freedom is gradually being transformed into the blessed impossibility of escaping from God's love. Already the heart senses that the battle against God's tenacious love is already lost. He is too near, and right now his love is so near that it takes away from us the fear that we, at the end, could still love something else besides just this love. When we run the course in this way, then we cannot find words glorious enough to praise the goal towards which we are hastening. For even our most clever illusions are punier than his reality, in which we will share. When we run the course in this way, then even the expectation of having spread out before us, on our last day, our whole life and all its possibilities, even the ones we neglected and refused, will not do us any harm. For in God's land there is no resignation. God will kiss all the tears from our cheeks; even the blessed tears of repentance will then not be too bitter for him. But how shall tears dry up and resignation change into laughter, if the neglected possibilities of life do not also become reality?

Let us therefore run forward, singing: it is good. Everything is good! And for him who runs to meet God nothing is past and lost forever. God has already bestirred himself and is quite near in the impatience of that love that makes all things new.

EXPERIENCING THE SPIRIT

The experience of the Spirit has nothing to do with any elitist consciousness of being one of the elect who are set apart from the great majority of average Christians and human beings. Experience of the Spirit occurs constantly in the life of anyone who is alive to personal self-possession and to the action of freedom, and truly in control of his entire self. In most human lives that does not happen as meditation proper, in self-immersive inward communion, and so on, but in the warp and weft of everyday life, where responsibility, loyalty, love and so on are practised absolutely, and where ultimately it is a secondary question whether such behaviour is accompanied by any expressly religious interpretation. That does not mean, however, that any such thematically religious interpretation is not correct and important in itself. Meditation and similar spiritual 'exercises' are not to be devalued. They can be a form of training for the occasion when ultimate experiences of the Spirit (wherever they occur in life) are accepted in radical, absolute freedom. Such exercises can also (though not exclusively) afford the opportunity to experience the Spirit more clearly and reflectively. They should be grasped in the ultimate fundamental freedom of the human being so that they become a decision comprising the whole of existence and taking it into salvation.

Christianity is not elitist. If we look at the New Testament, it offers details of various sublime experiences of the Spirit that can be summarized as 'mystical'. But all men who selflessly love their neighbour and experience God in that love are accorded ultimate salvation by God's jurisdiction, which is not capped by the highest assent or deepest immersion of the mystic. Therefore the New Testament, even when it does not expressly consider the point, is of the opinion that this insurpassable salvation in the self-communicating Holy Spirit of God can occur where apparently nothing more is happening than the final bitter duty of everyday life and a solitary death. Such an ultimate experience of the Spirit can occur in the midst of everyday life in spite of all the elitist pride of the 'pneumatics'.

Of course when there is genuine concern for salvation, and when God is loved, when a man learns ever more clearly that he can never come to a finally valid stop on the road of self-liberation, and when he submits to the hard though happy demands of the Sermon on the Mount, he will never refuse to take at least those expressly meditative and spiritual paths revealed to him in the ultimately inaccessible history of his life.

EVERYDAY MISSION

When we read the letters of Paul we eventually come upon his teaching about charismata, or charisms. These are not merely identical with a possession of the Spirit and the experience of the Spirit of a man justified by faith. But they do have an inward connexion with that possession of the Spirit and its form of experience. They are seen by Paul as versatile, always variously distributed capacities which are never all given to one individual; they are also comprise a commission to construct a Christian community. They may—like healing powers or speaking in tongues—be quite extraordinary and even spectacular in nature. But they can also be almost secular, everday capabilities, up to the point of good cash administration of a parish or community. In a sense we can overlook the importance of these charismata for the construction of the *community*. We may say that all abilities and possibilities, supported and ensouled by the Holy Spirit of God, are charismata or gifts of the Spirit.

Though we must not forget that the many separated Christians have in different ways one and the same possession of the Spirit, charismata are primarily quite sober individual commissions, individual abilities and individual offers, which make up the everydayness of a man and his many-sided life. Such possibilities always exceed what an individual man (given the limitations of his strength and time) can actually accomplish. He has to choose and discern. If he makes this choice duly (that is, in the Spirit and acting from the Spirit), then what is chosen may certainly be called 'charisma' or the 'will of God.'

How is such a choice made? The masters of the spiritual life have thought much about and experimented with the rules for the discernment of spirits, and have showed their conviction that the discovery of what is actually right here-

and-now is not *only* a matter for rational consideration and theoretical moral theology. Whenever such a choice of any specific thing is not merely rationally justified and does not merely accord with the principles of Christian morality, but also (something far from obvious) does not displace or darken an ultimate openness to specific experience of the Spirit in unlimited freedom, where a Christian experiences as given a final, non-arbitrary, rationally indissoluble yet factually given synthesis of original experience and the inclination to a specific object from his everyday freedom, then that Christian has found the will of God. Then he acts not only rationally and morally but charismatically. Of course a great deal of practice and spiritual experience are necessary in order to recognize accurately occasions when an inclination to a specific object proffered by everyday life does not displace this ultimate experience of the Spirit into an apparent void freed of God, but becomes the starting-point for that experience of the Spirit and offers a successful synthesis of the experience of the Spirit and everyday duties.

But the experience of such a synthesis, in which a man leaves everything for the unlimited mystery of God, in which his courageous decision 'fits' the actual reality of life and the 'world', is possible and comprises the whole Christian life. In such a life, with the dying Jesus, a man leaves everything in order to enter the exitless and unsignposted freedom of God, *and* at the same time lovingly accepts the individual everyday aspects of this world that are allotted him, in order to take them with him into that Spirit of God.

We must look for experience of the Spirit and for grace in the contemplation of our own lives. But not so that we can say, 'That's him. Now I know where the Spirit blows'. That is not how the Spirit is discerned. He cannot be found by laying triumphant claim to him as if he were our possession and property. We can seek him only by forgetting self. We can find him only in seeking God and surrendering self in generous outgoing love, and without returning to self. Moreover we must continually ask whether anything like that annihilating and enlivening experience of Spirit is at work in us, so that we know how far we still have to go, and how distant what we presume to call our 'spiritual' life still is from real experience of the Holy Spirit.

Grandis nobis restat vis. Venite et gustate, quam suavis sit Dominus! There is still a long way to go. Come and see how full the Lord is of loving-kindness!

UNITY OF THE CHURCH

Ultimately only one thing can give unity in the Church on the human level: the love which allows another to be different, even when it does not understand him. This makes it more understandable that charity is not only present in the Church as though in a container, but itself belongs to the actual constitutive elements of the Church, in contra-distinction to all other societies. For only then can the Church be one in spite of its dual structure. The principle that charity brings with it implies that each in the Church may follow his spirit as long as it is not established that he is yielding to what is contrary to the Spirit; that, therefore, orthodoxy, freedom and goodwill are to be taken for granted and not the opposite. Those are not only self-evident human maxims of a sensible common life built on respect and tolerance for others, but also principles which are very deeply rooted in the very nature of the Church and must be so. For they follow from the fact that the Church is not a totalitarian system. Patience, tolerance, leaving another

113

to do as he pleases as long as the error of his action is not established—and not the other way round, prohibition of all individual initiative until its legitimacy has been formally proved, with the onus of proof laid on the subordinate—are, therefore, specifically ecclesiastical virtues springing from the very nature of the Church.

We must learn, then, even as members of the Church, to let others be, even when we do not understand them, even when one has the 'feeling' that they don't think as one 'really' should, that is, according to one's own particular dispositions. It follows that there must be schools and trends in theology, in the spiritual life, in church art and in pastoral practice. Anyone who does not admit this is tacitly asserting that there could be a place in the Church from which all those matters were directed in detail, authoritatively, in a way binding on all and in all, so that all other persons would be merely the executors (and of a most passive and repetitive sort) of quite definite detailed views and commands. But that is just what is not the case. Even in theology it is not so; even, that is, in theory, which after all is more susceptible of unanimity than practical matters are. Of course, there are always naive and over-enthusiastic souls whose secret wish and ideal is, in fact, represented by what the opponents of papal infallibility at the time of the first Vatican Council always painted on the wall of their untheological imaginations as a nightmare danger, namely that the infallible pope might simply settle all theological questions by his infallible pronouncement. One should ask oneself for once just why, strictly speaking, that really will not do, seeing that after all he has authority for something of the sort. If one attentively considers the simple and rather foolish question, one realizes that it is really the case that the plenary powers of the highest authority in the Church, which are not subject to the check of any other human court of appeal, are not by any means the whole source from which, and in accordance with which, that highest authority acts. There belongs to it too the assistance of the Holy Spirit, which cannot be completely expressed in juridical terms, and his guidance in the actual exercise of those plenary powers. Moreover, in the present case it has to be noted too that human truth in fact is of such a kind that even in theology to settle one question, even correctly, raises three new questions that remain to be settled. Only simple-minded people fail to realize that, and think the pope, if he were only willing, could change dogmatic theology into a collection of defined propositions. For that matter it is only necessary to glance into church history to see that there has never been a trend in the Church which in the long run was wholly and solely right and triumphed to the exclusion of all others. And trends or programmes only put themselves completely in the wrong when they put themselves outside the Church in schism. One alone has always been completely right, the one Lord of the Church who, one in himself, has willed the many opposing tendencies in the Church.

MAN IS A MYSTERY

Man is a mystery. He is more than this. He is *the* mystery, not only because he is open to the mystery of the incomprehensible fulness of God, but also because God has expressed this mystery as his own. Assuming that God wanted to express himself in the empty void and that he wanted to call his Word into that void, how could he do anything other than create in man an inner hearing of his Word and express his Word in such a way that the self-expression of that Word and its being heard become one.

The fact that this indeed happens is itself a mystery. The unexpected, incalculable element that is both astonishing and self-evident (it is only self-evident because the mystery in the last resort makes the conceptual aspect understandable and not *vice versa*) is also a mystery. God's becoming man, then, is the absolute mystery and it is also self-evident. It is almost possible to imagine that the strange, historically contingent and hard aspect is not the reality in itself, but is the fact that this absolute and self-evident mystery has taken place, then and now, in Jesus of Nazareth. Our longing for the absolute nearness of God, which is incomprehensible in itself, but which makes it possible for us to endure everything, may, however, make us aware that this nearness is not to be found in the claims of the spirit, but in the flesh and here on earth. In that case, we shall find that proximity of God in no other place but in Jesus of Nazareth, above whom God's star is placed and before whom we can have the courage to kneel and pray: 'The Word was made flesh and dwelt among us'.

SOURCES

The Eternal Year
Encyclopedia of Theology
Meditations on Hope and Love
Christian at the Crossroads
Encounters with Silence
Servants of the Lord
Everyday Faith
Biblical Homilies
The Trinity
Hominization
On Heresy
Revelation and Tradition
Visions and Prophecies
Watch and Pray with Me
The Christian of the Future
The Religious Life Today
The Church and the Sacraments
The Dynamic Element in the Church
The Spirit in the Church
Sacramentum Mundi